If You Should Fail

A Book of Solace

JOE MORAN

VIKING
an imprint of
PENGUIN BOOKS

VIKING

UK | USA | Canada | Ireland | Australia
India | New Zealand | South Africa

Viking is part of the Penguin Random House group of companies
whose addresses can be found at global.penguinrandomhouse.com

Penguin
Random House
UK

First published 2020
001

Copyright © Joe Moran, 2020

The moral right of the author has been asserted

Set in 11/13 pt Dante MT Std
Typeset by Jouve (UK), Milton Keynes
Printed and bound in Great Britain by Clays Ltd, Elcograf S.p.A.

A CIP catalogue record for this book is available from the British Library

ISBN: 978–0–241–42279–3

www.greenpenguin.co.uk

For Jo

Contents

Despair Young and Never Look Back

Or why failure is not a lesson

All through that winter he was there. Every morning, as soon as I entered my office, I looked out of the window to check. A young rough sleeper had camped in an unused doorway of the hotel across the street from my university building – although *camped* rather oversells the nature of his sleeping arrangements.

He could hardly have alighted on a less suitable spot to lay his head. The doorstep on which he slept was about half the width of a child's single bed and about two-thirds the length of his body, which meant that he had to twist his spine to stay on it. The doorway had no porch, so his only defence against the elements was his sleeping bag. When it was cold and wet he just tried to sleep on, getting colder and wetter. Around ten, he wriggled out of his bag and, still dressed in his dirty combats and parka, stood up and shook himself down. Sometimes a kindly waiter fetched him some cold toast left over from the hotel breakfast, and he sat there munching it, slowly and sadly.

I work in an urban university, a former polytechnic made up of buildings acquired ad hoc and scattered around the centre of an English maritime city. There is no cloistered quadrangle here, hidden behind stone walls and a porters' lodge – not even a discrete campus. We are parked in the middle of the city's problems. Leaving work late one evening I found a man, half-sleeping and half-moaning, in the vestibule entrance. The leavings of other rough sleepers – cheap bivouacs, damp duvets, empty bottles – litter the route from my building to the car park. From my office I hear shouts in the street, people wailing bewilderedly at the world.

You learn to tune them out. Like most people, I deploy an efficient mental filter system to shut out the lives of others and, as the Chinese saying goes, 'watch the fire burn from the other side of the river'. But this young man had somehow filtered through. My office window just happened to be directly above and opposite the doorway where, of all the square feet of spare pavement in this city, he had chosen to sleep. We seemed linked by the accident of sight lines, even though he never once looked up at me. Each morning he played out this little urban parable for my benefit, as if his life were an Italian neorealist film and my window a cinema screen.

When not asleep, he was usually reading a book, although he was too far away for me to see what book it was. He would spend hours reading it before disappearing somewhere, leaving his sleeping bag and belongings behind. The next morning, when I entered my office, there he was again.

It shouldn't have made any difference. But for me that book fleshed him out, and made him seem more like one of the students I teach. It struck me that all he needed to turn him into one of them was an ID card with a barcode that would buzz him into the building. With one of those small oblong bits of PVC, bestowed when entry requirements are met and tuition fees paid, he could have entered the friendly functionalism of the classrooms, the calm of the library and the convivial hum of the cafe. He could have joined one of my classes and shared his thoughts about that dog-eared paperback in his hands. Instead he was out in the cold and wet of a northern English winter.

My own ID card fits in a plastic holder, attached to a braided lanyard worn around my neck. This is the magic entry ticket that, with a quick wrist-flick at the entrance scanner by the doors, turns me into persona grata. It lets me into a building where I have my own office, my own mug on a shelf in the staff kitchen, a pigeonhole with my name typed and stuck on with sticky tape, and people who know me and rely on me to show up. Getting through that door is my first and sometimes only success of the day. It tells me that I am a fit and proper person to enter a building – that I am not, on this rudimentary level, a failure.

Still, I know I am just another payroll number. Were I to displease my employer once too often, my lanyard would be seized and I would be out on the street, never again to hear that cheering open-sesame buzz. Watching that rough sleeper, it struck me how flimsy is the carapace of competence that makes us feel like paid-up members of the human race. I kept thinking of the first line of a Dana Spiotta novel: 'It is easy for a life to become unblessed.'

These young homeless people have multiplied on Britain's streets in recent years: human-shaped heaps of blankets, walled in by rucksacks, plastic carriers and cardboard layers. You find them in the covered entrances to supermarkets, the stairwells of car parks, the alcoved windows of department stores. Recently I passed an art exhibition on homelessness in the foyer of our university library. One exhibit was a single sheet of corrugated cardboard sculpted into the shape of a hooded man hunched foetally on the floor. No caption was provided, or needed.

Often it's hard to work out if there is a body inside them, these little mounds of rootless humanity. Sometimes you see a head half-poking out of the mound, asleep or with a lost, vacant look. Sometimes you don't, because the human occupant has absented themselves. The odd passer-by does a double take, briefly wondering if anyone is in there. Most walk by without a sideways glance. We all struggle to reinsert a whole person into that shape: someone with a name, a family, a life history that led them here and a body just as achy and sore as yours would be if your mattress were a pavement, your roof the open sky and your only shelter the lintel of a door that never opens for you.

3

A month or so after that young man started bedding down in that hotel doorway, another rough sleeper, a Hungarian called Gyula Remes, collapsed and died in central London. Homeless EU nationals rarely sought help to get off the streets because government policy, until the High Court ruled it illegal, had been to deport them. At forty-three, Remes had died a year short of the mean age at death of a homeless person in England. He was the second man in a year to die in the underpass leading from Westminster tube station to the Houses of Parliament, a spot where homeless people would gather – until, a few months after his death, rolldown shutters were installed and drove them out.

Shocking, perhaps, that MPs could walk so casually past the visible effects of austerity. But not, perhaps, surprising – since they are no different from the rest of us, we who avert our eyes from this daily calamity playing out on the other side of a pavement. Those who live on the streets feel unseen, expelled from humankind. That is why so many of them sound soft-voiced and chastened, and others so aggrieved. To be viewed as this kind of failure, and not some official category of victim deserving of charity and pity, is to be a pariah. Ending one's life as a pile of rags on the street, a mound of indeterminate humanness for others to walk round, is worse than heartbreaking. It is humiliating.

The story we tell ourselves about homelessness is so often about the failures of its victims. A rough sleeper, we imagine, must have done something foolish or self-destructive – involving drink, drugs or a family bust-up, perhaps – to lead them to this pitiful place. Far easier to label someone a failure than to join the dots that link us to them. Subtly and noxiously, the thought overtakes us – that their failure is a matter of personal failings, that the ruined have, in calm seas, shipwrecked themselves.

The foundational myth of failure is that it's our own fault. Failure for the ancient Greeks was the result of hubris, the human defiance of the gods, a defiance met by the avenging goddess Nemesis. Icarus drowns in the Mediterranean because he gets above himself, flying too close to the sun with his waxen wings. Sisyphus is punished for his deceit by having to push a rock up a hill for ever. In our oldest stories, plagues, poor harvests and barren wombs arrive not as chance calamities but as judgements of the gods.

Hubris and Nemesis mutated into the religious idea of sin and damnation, or those laws of cosmic balance which demand that bad acts be costed and accounted for in this life or the next. The Hindu notion of karma employs a tariff derived from the nature of the offence. A slanderer is reborn with halitosis, a heavy drinker with blackened teeth, a thief with no possessions and a gossip as someone no one believes, even when they speak the truth.

This human hunger for stories, the need to turn life into allegory, is not just a religious urge. Even in the mostly godless world I inhabit, victims are still thought to deserve their lot, and often blame themselves. Successful people still fear that they will have to pay a bill of bad luck later on to restore equity. Behind this fallacy of a just world lies the illusion of control. We need to feel that we have some say over the unseeable course of our lives. The world, we like to imagine, cares what happens to us; when we find that it doesn't, we decide that we have let the world down. Better to think that a vengeful god has punished us than that we are alone in an infinite and uncaring universe.

A truer account of failure appears in the Old Testament's Book of Job. Job is the unluckiest man in the land of Uz. Fire, winds and marauding mobs of Sabeans and Chaldeans take away all his livestock, his servants and his children, and then, when he still blesses the Lord's name, he suffers 'loathsome sores from the sole of his foot to the crown of his head'. Three of Job's friends – Eliphaz, Bildad and Zophar – arrive. These 'friends' insist that to deserve such ruin he must have drawn God's wrath. But Job has done nothing wrong; God is only showing off His omnipotence. Job accepts that 'the Lord gave, and the Lord hath taken away'. At the end of the book, as a reward for this stoicism, God restores Job to his fortunate life – blessing him with beautiful daughters and renewed wealth – as cursorily as He took it away.

Failure struts its stuff like that Old Testament God. Just like the Christian concept of grace, failure is unearned and conferred on the deserving and undeserving alike. Like God's grace, it has no truck with fairness: *There, but for the grace of God, go I.* It does its faceless and nameless work on whoever gets in its way. Those of us who have avoided its line of path, for now, act like Job's comforters and find some explanation for why this isn't happening to us, or worry that we may be next.

One of Sigmund Freud's great discoveries was that feelings of shame have little to do with actual wrongdoing and much to do with our fear of losing the love of others. The shame of failure is contagious, self-replicating and reality-distorting. It can be passed around interminably and uselessly, leaving mental havoc in its wake. We look away from rough sleepers because we fear that what they suffer from is catching – that they host this deadly pathogen, failure, that they might pass on to us. Meanwhile we try to build up immunity to the pathogen by accumulating reserves of its universal antibody: success.

It can't be done. In her book *Precarious Life*, Judith Butler argues that human beings are tied tightly to one another, even those we have never met, through our shared vulnerability. Just occupying a soft, malleable, mortal body makes us vulnerable, she writes. Our skin and flesh expose us not only to other people's germs but to their love, their desire, their anger, their violence and their gaze. Human beings are inescapably social creatures, made of need. We can be wounded, or enraptured, by the merest glance or nod from another member of our species. Butler calls this shared vulnerability our *precariousness*.

The Bantu languages of southern Africa have another word

for it: *ubuntu*. *Ubuntu* is not easy to translate. But its gist is that your selfhood is borrowed from and lent to others, that you become a person through other people, that you are diminished when they are diminished. Your life is not simply your own. Each self is leaky and permeable, part of other selves. Your failures belong to everyone else, as everyone else's belong to you. We complete each other.

We can no more escape failure than protect ourselves entirely from any other contagion, and for the same reason: no one ever made themselves immune to other people. We like to see ourselves as sovereign entities that succeed or fail under their own steam. Failure is the virus we hope never to catch, but it has too many strains for us to escape it indefinitely. Sooner or later, in the chickenpox party of life, everyone catches failure from everyone else.

I too must have feared that the failure of that rough sleeper was contagious – for as the weeks passed I never once walked across to help him. I excused my inertia with the usual self-forgiving fatalism. There was little I could do, I told myself, when he wasn't asking for help, or even anyone's spare change.

Eventually I looked up a nearby night shelter on the web. Its volunteers did sweeps of the streets and invited rough sleepers to a warm dorm with free roll mats. I rang them up, gave them his coordinates, and the next day he was gone. A single phone call had allayed my useless guilt, no distressing interaction required. Now, removed from my sight, he was someone else's problem – someone else's failure.

But that young man and I were not so different. As I watched him through my window, I was fairly sure of one thing: both of us felt like failures. A year's worth of my work had just come decisively to nothing. None of it could be salvaged or reused; all I could do was walk away and move on. As often happens when we fail, I began to rehearse in my head all the other failures in my life. Thus sliced and spliced in my brain's cutting room by that control-freakish auteur, the superego, this life seemed to read like one long story of unsuccess.

I had not been hubristic or sinful like Icarus or Sisyphus. Nor could my failure be reframed as heroic. It bore no resemblance to that ideal of romanticized failure associated with British army generals making doomed cavalry charges, or male American writers burning brightly in youth and washed up in early middle age. No such tragic nobility or poetic self-martyrdom clung to me. I had not drunk my talents away or misspent them on ego trips and folies de grandeur. I had worked assiduously away as usual, like the keen-to-please, first-hand-up-in-class boy I have always been. And still I had failed. In start-up business speak, I had *achieved failure*, completing a project diligently only to find that no one wanted the merchandise.

For some reason this made the loss of time and effort more shaming. I had nothing and no one to blame. The failure was not my fault, or anyone's fault. Nor did it have any consequence, except in my own head. My year's worth of wasted work was of no concern to anyone else. No public disgrace or penance ensued; no one liked me any less.

My failure seemed nugatory when compared to that rough sleeper's misery. Mine had not been a cursed or beleaguered life – just a bog-standard, ambition-thwarted, award-losing one, with all the normal midlife stuff about missed chances and wrong turnings. Move along, now; nothing to see. I knew that talking myself up as a failure would seem to others like reverse arrogance, implying that I didn't think I had received my rightful share of success. And I also knew that on the upper slopes of that thought lies the delusional bitterness which is its own kind of failure. Most failure is felt alone. When we dump its untranslatable emotional states on others, we can hardly blame them for seeing it as bad manners.

Yet the failure is real enough. 'We share our lives with the people we have failed to be,' the psychotherapist Adam Phillips has written.[1] When we fail, we mourn those unlived lives – the loss of something we never had and never were, except in our imaginings. We grieve for what never died because it never existed. We feel like failures when we fall down the yawning gap between our aspirations and our achievements. Worse than plain disappointment, failure exposes our dreams as dead ends. It is a mortifying reckoning with the complacent fictions we have built around ourselves.

Around the turn of the millennium, many first-generation internet entrepreneurs fell victim to the dotcom crash. They had built market share by offering free services online, hoping to make a profit from them later. Share values rose untenably – a classic stock-market bubble. The bubble burst, as bubbles do, and the start-ups went bust. By the time their founders re-emerged in the mid 2000s with new ventures, they had rebadged their losses as a lesson. At pop-up events such as FailCon and FuckUp Nights, they shared their stories of failure and what it had taught them. In the new Wild West of Silicon Valley, they were retelling an American myth – of the frontier spirit that carried the pioneers through the hard miles across the continent, before they struck crude oil or the Comstock Lode. Ancient myths recount the same tale of a hero on an epic journey, who is tested to his limits and changed for ever. The hero succeeds by persevering in the face of failure.

A venture-backed start-up doesn't yet know who its customers are or what they want; its task is to find out quickly before the money runs out. Better, then, to realize early on that an idea isn't working. Fail fast, fail early, fail often. Fail with a soft landing. Learn your mistakes with your first company and start again. In Silicon Valley, the colossal rewards of success make such failure a tolerable risk – even if, in the real world that techies call 'meatspace', failure still means investors losing money and employees losing their jobs.

This ethos of 'failing well' soon spread beyond the world of tech. In 2011, the *Harvard Business Review* devoted a whole issue to 'the F word'. American colleges began running courses on impostor syndrome, perfectionism and coping with failure. The personal growth industry grew its own sub-industry of failure wisdom – books on *the gift of failure* and *the up side of down*, and those motivational talks where the speaker bestrides the stage with a headset mic and no notes, telling you that success starts with failure.

We can learn from our failures – sometimes. And saying so is better, I suppose, than the machismo of 'failure is not an option' – a phrase I have always heard as inviting the very thing it forbids just by mentioning it, rather like the self-cancelling command 'Don't think of an elephant.' But the failing well movement too often succumbs to platitudinous positivity. It is a symptom of our new Promethean age, with its blind faith in the permanent reinvention of the self. Behind the cute refrains – *Failure is your greatest teacher, Make failure your fuel, Turn your failure into fodder* – lies the wishful thinking of alchemy, where the base metal of failure always turns into golden accomplishment.

In the middle of my own season of failure, I kept seeing illuminated poster adverts for a pop musician's autobiography, with a line from the book. 'Those years when I took a dive and I lost control,' it read, 'maybe they were worth it because the way I'd put myself back together might just be a better me.' This advert seemed to follow me around, at bus stops and railway stations. I started to take it personally. It felt odd to be lectured on failure by someone so successful that his bromides were backlit in bus shelters.

I had no wish to turn my failure into a life lesson, especially since it seemed, as Freudians say, so 'overdetermined' – with multiple and interpenetrating causes, any of which would have been enough for failure to occur. I did not want to hear that *failure makes perfect* or *failure is delay not defeat* or *failure defeats losers and inspires winners* or *failure is a bruise not a tattoo.* If we only look at failure like this, through the rear-view mirror of the successful, then its merits will be inflated and its pain trivialized.

The day after a British scientist won the Nobel Prize for medicine, one of his old rejection letters from the journal *Nature* began circulating on social media, posted with suitably boosterish comments. *Believe in yourself,* they said. *Everyone else will catch up eventually. Success will find you in the end. Failure is the stepping stone to success.*

Except that none of this is true. Believing in yourself will not always make people believe in you. Success will not always find you in the end. Failure is not always the stepping stone to success. The most concerted efforts misfire; the most gilded life is left with wrecked dreams and useless regrets. In any race, most of us will be also-rans. Failure is always odds-on. It is statistical probability, basic maths, a numbers game – reversion to the norm.

Ever tried. Ever failed. No Matter. Try again. Fail again. Fail better. Over the last few years, Samuel Beckett's words have congealed into cliché. You see them on tea towels, hoodies, mugs and iPhone covers. Richard Branson quoted them in a piece he wrote about Virgin's entrepreneurial mindset, adding that they 'could just as easily come from the mouth of yours truly'. The tennis player Stan Wawrinka had them tattooed on his left arm. In 2014, the Harvard Business School published *Fail Better: Design Smart Mistakes and Succeed Sooner,* a book about how to ensure that 'every failure is maximally useful' by developing a 'fail better mindset'.

Beckett would surely have hated that word *mindset* as much as I do. I don't want my mind to be set, successfully or otherwise. I want it to be porous, pliable, persuadable – even if that means sometimes seeming half-hearted or irresolute. Anything else feels like a failure of the imagination.

All this is Beckett's fault, partly. He once briefly flirted with a career as an advertising copywriter and he had an ear for word jingles and sticky syntax that hung around in the head. The 'fail better' quote comes from his brief, late work, *Worstward Ho*. In context – a surrounding prose of tired repetitions and verbless sentences – the words read rather differently. Not that you need to read them in context; you just need to know slightly more than nothing about Samuel Beckett.

As a young man, Beckett was a star. He captained his school at cricket and rugby, and at Trinity College Dublin won prizes and scholarships. He got the top first in his year, graduating with a gold medal in modern literature. After a spell teaching at the École normale supérieure in Paris, the finishing school for the French intellectual elite, he was appointed to a lectureship at Trinity, aged twenty-four.

But Beckett the lecturer saw himself as an impostor. He thought it ludicrous to be teaching others what he barely knew himself. He came down with a host of psychosomatic ailments – headaches, cysts, insomnia – and resigned from his job after little over a year. He wrote casually to a friend about the 'charming little cunt of a gold medallist' who would replace him.[2] But this hid the deep remorse he felt at letting down his family, who had been so proud of his success – especially his father, who died eighteen months later, a death Beckett never got over.

From then on, Beckett followed the advice he once scribbled in a note to the writer Aidan Higgins: 'Despair young and never look back.'[3] He spent days curled up in bed in the dark, facing the wall, the covers over his head. His first book, *Dream of Fair to Middling Women*, was rejected by every publisher he sent it to and did not appear until after his death. The book he salvaged from it, *More Pricks than Kicks*, sold just a few hundred copies. His next, *Murphy*, was accepted by the forty-third publisher he tried.

'To be an artist is to fail,' Beckett wrote in 1949. 'Failure is his world and the shrink from it desertion, art and craft, good housekeeping.' He was next to unknown until his late forties, when the slow-burn success of *Waiting for Godot* arrived. He still felt more at home with failure, he said, having all his writing life 'breathed deep of its vivifying air'.[4]

Beckett's work circles continually around the theme of failure: the failure of our bodies to do our bidding, the failure of words to fill the silence and confusion between us, the failure of a life to be more than a heap of desultory moments, the failure of others to notice our suffering when the noise of their own drowns it out. For Beckett, life is mainly filling time before our certain doom. Life is like the endgame, the final part of a chess game where the losing player struggles through their dying moves before the inevitable checkmate. 'You're on earth,' cries Hamm in *Endgame*, 'there's no cure for that!'

Is 'fail better' sounding less like an inspirational quote yet? *Worstward Ho*'s working title was *Better Worse*. Beckett took his cue from Edgar's speech in *King Lear*: 'The worst is not / So long as we can say "This is the worst." ' The 'fail better' quote is, like so much of Beckett's writing, a litany. It repeats and loops back, failing to move forward, like a stalled and stuttering human life. 'Fail better' doesn't mean 'keep trying', or even 'fail a little less catastrophically next time'. It means you must bear to go on, hauling your body into each new day, when you know that you will fail and fail again. 'Plod on and never recede,' as some less famous lines from *Worstward Ho* have it. 'Slowly with never a pause plod on and never recede.'[5]

And so Beckett's tote-bag-friendly phrase has itself failed, for 'fail better' is now read as the inverse of its intended meaning. Always anticipating failure, and at heart a comedian, Beckett would no doubt have found this amusing. Asked by *The Times* for his New Year's resolutions for that ominous year, 1984, he replied in a telegram: 'Resolutions: zero. Hopes: zero.'[6]

An old Yiddish proverb goes: 'Poverty is no disgrace – which is the only good thing you can say about it.' The same goes for failure. It's nothing to be ashamed of, but nothing to celebrate either. Mostly it's just a waste of time, something none of us mortals ever has enough of. No one should have to endure this waste of time and then be compelled to listen to a sermon on how good failure is for the soul. If failure can only be entertained as the rocket boost that propels us to greatness, then we are no longer talking about failure at all.

The duty to fail well is sentimental. Like all sentimentality, it converts unsoothing specificity into soothing abstraction. It meets the lonely-making ache of actual failure with a universalizing pro forma. It helps us not at all with the difficult, unanswerable questions about failure – such as when to get back on the horse that threw us, when to get on a different horse, and when to give up horse riding altogether.

The failing well movement claims to bust the stigma attached to failing. But failure is still right there, just where we left it. In today's paper, I read a story about a former soap star who has 'landed herself a new role' as a security guard at a discount supermarket. It belongs to a now well-established genre of tabloid story about once-famous actors spotted doing bar work or bagging groceries at checkouts. The story never points out that acting is an insecure profession. It never concedes that a freelance life often means taking on other work to pay the bills and buy food. It never suggests that this might be a necessary, even noble act. The inference is clear: a soap star working as a security guard is a failure.

Shame still attaches to failure as it ever has. That is why we are so quick to turn it into something else, to escape from its shame with stories of salvation. We should learn to live with failure for a little while. It might make us think about what success really amounts to, and why it is rarely the answer to our problems that we mistook it for.

Success divides us. In search of it, we drive through our lives in little armoured tanks of ego. Inside these tanks, we try to do two irreconcilable things: compete with others and win their approval and love. Failure strips us of all that competitive bullet plate. It makes us tender and undefended, more open to the world and each other. It teaches us what it means to be human – that is, fallible, non-algorithmic, full of quixotic plans and enlivening faults. It throws us off the hamster wheel of other people's expectations. It inspires modesty, compassion and an awareness that life is a crapshoot and there are numberless ways of living it well. Failure is not the dark obverse, the photographic negative of success, but its own abundant reality. It is knowledge, all the more salutary for being unsolicited.

In his poem 'Song of Myself', Walt Whitman sings 'vivas to those who have fail'd'. For all the world's failures, he promises a 'meal equally set'. When Whitman wrote this poem, he was also a failure, unsure of his future and by most outward signs a layabout. It begins as a hymn to the indomitable ego: 'I celebrate myself.' But it becomes a hymn to the great theatre of human belonging that is failure.

Failure is easier to deal with, I think, when it turns from a present into a past participle. To be *failing* is to be hurtling scarily in free fall; but to have *failed*, to have plumbed the depths and know that one cannot fall further, is not so bad. When failure bottoms out into something definitive and unarguable, it starts to bleed insights. We stop picking at our narcissistic wounds, which are so painful to us and so trivial to others, and begin to see failure not as our own secret disgrace, or as a disease that the careless may catch from the afflicted, or as a spur to self-improvement, but as a source of solidarity with billions of other failed souls.

This book is for anyone who has ever said to themselves *I am a failure*. I make appointments with all, as Whitman wrote, and turn no one away. Self-declared failure will suffice, no questions asked, whatever external symptoms of success you might exhibit.

Sometimes the only person whose opinion counts is the one saying *I am a failure*. Failure is a feeling, not an accreditation – and it should never, ever be a competition.

Just say it. *I am a failure*. A therapist might pull you up on that use of the verb *to be*, with its suggestion of non-negotiable permanence. But doesn't the word *failure*, with its soft consonants and long, liquid vowels, have a consoling quality – so unlike the clipped, self-assured sibilants of *success*? Only the incurably bumptious say *I am a success*. But lots of people say, as you are saying now, *I am a failure*.

To those who have failed, which is all of us, I offer no advice, only solace. Solace: from the Latin *solari*, to soothe. Solace is the reverse of what Job's comforters offered. It neither asks its recipient to learn from their distress nor lectures them on the reasons for it. It begins by accepting the reality of failure, because any attempt to console that ignores reality will make us feel worse in the end.

Solace is the antidote to what the critic Laurent Berlant calls 'cruel optimism'. Certain kinds of optimism are crueller than pessimism because they ask us to invest in a future that is at best unlikely and at worst a fantasy. Solace, by contrast, calls things for what they are. It lets us feel like failures without jabbing us in the ribs with the shallow certainties of positive thinking. Solace is not a rescue remedy. In place of cruel optimism it substitutes humane fatalism. It sees failure as a condition we share with the rest of the human race, as prosaic as walking upright and twiddling our opposable thumbs.

Solace offers no cure – only words. Yet words wield great power; they are probably what made you feel like a failure in the first place. 'No words,' people say nowadays, after something has happened that is meant to have defeated the possibilities of language. But there are always words, and we can always come up with better ones. And when people respond to other people's failures with well-hewn phrases that are neither truisms nor evasions, they tend to cut through.

If you should fail, and you will, I hope the words below provide some solace. Words of solace should offer not just comfort but cheer. An early sense of the word *solace*, now obsolete, was pleasure, amusement, delight. I would like my own words of solace to be cheering, too – but not at the expense of the truth. The most lasting solace comes from looking level-eyed at failure and staring it down, not looking straight past it with pep talks and pithy sayings. Despair young and never look back, I say. Plod on and never recede. Comrades in failure: onwards!

2.

Not Enough, Not Enough

Or why you feel like an impostor

In Aesop's fable 'The Fox and the Grapes', the grapes hang high up on a vine. The hungry fox leaps with all his strength to try and reach them, before giving up. He consoles himself with the thought that they were unripe and tart, and not worth eating. 'Sour grapes', the dead metaphor that derives from this fable, is now used to accuse someone of being a sore loser. But 'sour grapes' in Aesop stands for something quite different. It means to dismiss as worthless what we can't have. The grapes in the fable aren't really sour. Nor is the fox, who has rationalized his failure very well. Aesop's moral is that 'there are many who pretend to despise and belittle what is beyond their reach'. But the fox's attitude has always struck me as healthy – much better, surely, than moaning about what might have been.

I suffer from yet another kind of 'sour grapes'. I am the fox who reached the grapes and found that they really do taste sour. With boundless ingenuity, I explain away any small success I have and find some post hoc rationale for painting myself as a fraud. I cheapen success at the moment it arrives. If the grapes were so easy to reach with my feeble leap, I decide, then they can't be worth eating.

There may also be a trace of magical thinking in my secretly hoping for success in the face of intense visions of failure. If my hard work pays off, I retrospectively see these visions as an essential ingredient of my success. I only reached those grapes, I decide, because I worried that I wouldn't. Thus does any achievement become superstitiously linked with pre-emptive thoughts of failure. The moral of this alternative Aesop's fable is that humans, unlike foxes, have evolved a bottomless capacity for self-abasement.

Success always feels like a thing apart from me, never fully owned, easily explained away by chance or clerical error. Success is the fake tan, the radiant sheen I have acquired, and failure the pasty face exposed via a painful process of unpeeling. Success is the aberration, failure the elemental self. Success is the welcome stranger and failure the unwelcome familiar, the daemon I may no more escape from than part company with my shadow. When failure comes along, I think: *You again.*

In an essay about her brief career as a debating champion, Sally Rooney writes: 'Success doesn't come from within; it's given to you by other people, and other people can take it away.' While a student at Trinity College Dublin, Rooney toured Europe, conducting artfully contrived debates with groups of competitors from other countries. In 2013, aged twenty-two, she came first in the European Universities Debating Championships. She loved the buzz of competition, of hitting a perfect rhythm while speaking, going off on an impromptu riff like a jazz musician, plucking a killer point out of thin air to crush an opponent.

But a debating contest, she came to see, is an Olympics of impostordom. You must pretend to care deeply about your assigned topic and hide the fact that you may not even agree with yourself. 'Maybe I stopped debating,' Rooney writes, 'to see if I could still think of things to say when there weren't any prizes.'[1] Success feels like a sham because we crave and solicit it from others. The pursuit of it means relinquishing control over our lives.

My job, in which I am paid to perform academic authority, demands imposture. I used to get a dopamine hit from pulling off the performance and not being found out. I enjoyed inhabiting the omniscient, hyper-professional voice of a scholarly paper or making authoritative-sounding noises and gestures while stood behind a lectern. Lecturers lecture, professors profess. Mansplaining is in the job spec. But it always felt as if I were performing a trick and, after a while, faking it stopped being fun. I got tired of hearing my own voice blether on or watching my sentences shape themselves into the same worn-out moves. I did grasp that some kind of skill was involved as well – but no more, perhaps, than that of the lyrebird in captivity who can mimic so uncannily the sound of a chainsaw or a ringtone.

I have a recurring thought that, for all my students know, I could have wandered in off the street to teach them, like those con artists who pretend to be surgeons and perform operations or who fake a pilot's licence and fly passenger jets. It is no use telling myself how unlikely this sounds. People do not, generally, pretend to be university lecturers – partly because, once you are in front of a class, there are no other decision-makers around, such as anaesthetists or co-pilots, from whom you might discreetly solicit help. Real-life impostors also like to spin grandiose fantasies of power and authority – and dressing up in surgical scrubs or a pilot's uniform is a more glamorous gig than sneaking into classrooms to give lectures on contemporary poetry.

One of the set pieces of the medical memoir comes when the newly qualified doctor is sent on to the wards, sleep-deprived and unready, to do their best or worst. A newly minted PhD, likewise, is given a room and some students and told to fill a few hours. The stakes of success or failure are lower. We perform no life-saving procedures. No one bleeps us in an emergency. If we do any good, the effects are hidden and long deferred. But medics and lecturers are similar in one respect: they are both playing a role and often come to feel like impostors. 'A teacher affects eternity; he can never tell where his influence stops,' wrote Henry Adams. But he can never tell where it starts, either. Teaching means passing on something evanescent and immeasurable to a group of near strangers. Most of the time, like most things worth doing, it ends in failure.

If only my students knew, while I radiate professorial competence, that I finished writing this lecture an hour ago and am only a fortnight ahead of them with the course reading. If only my academic peers knew that this breastplate of carefully caveated argument and footnotery hid a bruisable skin of self-doubt and confusion. Scholarly research can go on for months with little obvious sign of progress – bad news for self-appointed impostors. Even when finished, it is meant to be provisional and falsifiable, so someone can come along to point at the holes in our argument or the groundbreaking paper we failed to read.

Academia is a finessing, fault-finding culture, where there is always another reference to check, another source to chase up, another theory to take on board. Most of the feedback we get is critique; unqualified praise is rare and viewed, I have long suspected, as vulgar. Scholars are taught instead to admire 'critical thinking' – an unending sceptical vigilance about the capacity to know anything at all. We are always one slip from being exposed for ever as frauds.

In January 1897, at the age of thirty-two, Max Weber was appointed to a prestigious chair at the University of Heidelberg. A brilliant and prolific scholar, he had already held two previous professorships. He inherited his punishing work ethic from his father, a government official with whom he had tortured relations, and who died shortly after he moved to Heidelberg. When Weber's friends warned him about his workload, he replied that if he could not work at this rate he had no right to be called a scholar.

Early that summer, Weber began weeping for hours at a time – the first sign of a slow-moving breakdown. For the next two years he struggled to fulfil his teaching duties. By the end of 1898 he was so worn out that he collapsed when trimming the Christmas tree. Even reading a newspaper upset him. The only things that calmed him down a little were modelling figures in wax and playing with children's building blocks. He became hypersensitive to noise and irritable at the slightest cause. The cat's meowing drove him so mad that his wife, Marianne, gave it away. By the summer of 1900, according to Marianne, 'everything was too much for him; he could not read, write, talk, walk, or sleep without torment. All his mental and some of his physical functions failed him.'

Weber entered a clinic for nervous diseases in the spa town of Bad Urach. This former workaholic now spent days just lying in the garden or walking in the Swabian Alps. Marianne took him on a long holiday to southern Italy, Corsica, Rome and Switzerland – to no avail. She called her husband 'a chained Titan whom evil, envious gods were plaguing'.

For three years he did no reading, writing or teaching. Just the thought of marking a student's essay requiring major rewriting or turning up to give a lecture at a set time paralysed him. It also filled him with shame that he was now in receipt of a salary for doing nothing. Twice he handed in his resignation to Heidelberg and it was refused. Finally, in October 1903, after four years of sick leave, it was accepted. 'In the prime of his life,' Marianne wrote, 'Weber found himself expelled from his kingdom.'[2]

He was, however, at last emerging from his torpor and returning to writing. He wanted to understand why his high-achieving life had crippled him with such guilt and fear. He began thinking about the relationship between modern capitalism and compulsive labour.

In his 1905 essay *The Protestant Ethic and the Spirit of Capitalism*, Weber argued that a new attitude to work had emerged after the Reformation, among ascetic Protestant sects in England, Holland and New England. This new ethic had turned money-making, once considered a sin, into a sign of God's grace. Weber traced this doctrinal shift back to the sixteenth-century theologian John Calvin. Calvin rejected the traditional Catholic cycle of sin, repentance and atonement. Instead he focused on the elect, the strictly limited number of mortals already earmarked to be saved from eternal hellfire.

Weber was interested in how a seventeenth-century English disciple of Calvin, Richard Baxter, had revised his thinking. Baxter sought to mitigate Calvin's fatalism, his belief that we are always already saved or damned to hell. Baxter thought that our efforts in this life could still please our Maker and that the earth existed for His glorification. Work tamed the base and bestial side of human nature, and made God's earthly Kingdom prosper. A pious life was an active life, and time-wasting a sin.

In this post-Calvinist theology, sinful mortals still did not know whom God had elected to save. But until the Day of Judgement, they could at least seek to prove their virtue before an all-seeing, silent God, and look for signs of God's grace in their daily lives. They could serve God by working hard, and that could involve making money. Calvinism's asceticism, though, discouraged use of that money for trivial, worldly pleasures. Profits had to be reinvested to benefit God's community.

For Weber, capitalism is driven by this constant search for more profits, fresh markets, further growth. It never sleeps. It works by accumulating wealth rather than just meeting our immediate needs – and wealth can be accumulated, and worldly pleasures deferred, without end. The profit motive is an infinitely demanding God. It makes us permanently dissatisfied with ourselves. The workaholics who worry that they are impostors are seeking to prove themselves one of the elect, but no amount of work will ever feel enough. They are trying to answer Calvinism's unanswerable question: will I be saved?

The Italian writer Natalia Ginzburg thought herself an impostor all her life. She was born Natalia Levi in 1916, the youngest of five children. Her father, Giuseppe Levi, professor of anatomy at the University of Turin, was an overbearing patriarch who took a cold shower at four each morning, breakfasted on home-made yoghurt, ran to work at dawn and scolded his sons for not doing as well as he did at school. The young Natalia was surrounded by such confident, driven men. If she spoke at the dinner table, her three older brothers shushed her and carried on talking.

Until the age of eleven, she was schooled at home, but her tutors made her fall asleep. She didn't understand arithmetic and failed to learn her times tables. She couldn't knit, dress herself, tie her shoelaces or make the bed. She wasn't sporty. Her parents saw her as a lost cause and, like most children stamped in such a way, she came to agree with them. As a young woman, she befriended the anti-fascist intellectuals who gathered in her family's sitting room in Turin, such as Adriano Olivetti, Cesare Pavese, Carlo Levi and Leone Ginzburg, whom she married in 1938. She listened in a corner as these clever, animated young men set about fixing the world with their words. At seventeen, she failed exams in Latin, Greek and maths. She never took a degree, dropping out of the University of Turin after again failing Latin.

Then, in a few short years, tragedy entered her life and stayed there. Her Jewish father was stripped of his academic post and briefly imprisoned, before fleeing to Belgium. Two of her brothers were jailed as members of the resistance; the third escaped from the fascist police by swimming across the River Tresa to Switzerland. In 1940, her husband, Leone, who had already been jailed for two years for anti-fascism, was sentenced to *confino*, or 'restricted residence', in the village of Pizzoli in the wild Abruzzi region. She and their three young children went with him. In 1943, with the Germans occupying half the country and arresting Jews, Leone fled to Rome. Natalia and their children followed on under false names. Leone was then seized by the Nazis for running an underground newspaper. In February 1944, in Rome's Regina Coeli prison, they tortured him to death.

These horrors might have added perspective and proportion to Ginzburg's girlish sense of herself as a failure. In fact, encountering real loss in early adulthood made little difference to her adolescent feelings of inadequacy. Most of us imagine that grief, when it comes, will clarify. It will take us out of the normally worrisome world into a new place, painful but clean and clear, like the thinnest mountain air, where triumph and disaster will seem like twin impostors. This fails to happen. When grief arrives, it just leaves the world as it is, only messier and more mystifying for having to navigate this blue fog of shock and pain on top.

Grief does not soften our feelings of failure – but it may, as Ginzburg found, make them less self-absorbed. She wrote later that, while she had encountered much human brutality during the war, what made the pain hardest to bear was the insouciance of fate, its unconcern at our plight. Fate teaches us that failure is nothing personal, and that we will all be its victims in the end.

In one of her essays, on 'Fantasy Life', she argues that in our youth feeling sorry for ourselves yields 'rich, voluptuous feelings'. But in adulthood, the retaining wall between reality and dream cracks and then collapses. Our vivid fantasy life, where we turned into more lovable versions of ourselves, evaporates. We learn that our daydreams will not protect us from the inexorability of time and chance. For Ginzburg, the writer's life is a gradual journey from invention to memory, from imagination to truth. And the truth we learn is that life owes us nothing and that sometimes, for no good reason, we just fail.

In October 1944, aged twenty-eight, the newly widowed Ginzburg came back to liberated Rome to find work. She got a job at the publishing house Einaudi, but felt, perhaps rightly, that she was only there because she and her late husband had been friends of its founder, Giulio Einaudi. In her essay 'Laziness', she carefully itemizes her general uselessness around this time. She had no degree and had never been able to finish any projects. She knew no languages except a little French and could not type. And she lost 'an infinite amount of time idling and daydreaming'.

She was certain that the minute she entered the office everyone would discover 'the vast sea of ignorance and laziness inside me'. To guard against this, in that unwinnable game that all impostorists play, she 'worked furiously, dizzily, immersed in total isolation'. She even had a key cut so that she could let herself into the office on Sundays. Before long she found that she had completed the Italian translations of Nadezhda Krupskaya's *Memories of Lenin*, Johan Huizinga's *Homo Ludens* and the first two volumes of Proust.

In the summer just after the war, Ginzburg resorted to psychoanalysis. But this too left her feeling inadequate. One day she told her psychoanalyst that she could never manage to fold blankets neatly. He went to fetch a blanket. He made her fold it, which she did, and to show willing she said she had mastered it, even though she knew she had not. Shortly afterwards, she stopped seeing him. Far from assuaging her feelings of failure, her psychoanalysis had become 'one of the numerous things I had started and not finished because of my disorganization, ineptitude, and confusion'.

Failure, to mean a person who has failed, is of fairly recent coinage. The *Oxford English Dictionary* dates it to only 1865. Before then, the historian Scott Sandage notes, the word was 'an incident, not an identity'. A *failure* meant a business that had failed. Failure first became an identity, Sandage argues, in nineteenth-century America.

The American economy in this period settled into a pattern of boom and bust, dependent on the whims of the big New York banks and investors. This delivered a major crash every two decades or so, from the Panic of 1819 to the depression of the mid 1890s. Just as small businessmen became less in control of their destinies, a new vocabulary emerged to brand them as self-made failures. Credit-rating agencies, which opened in the 1840s, supplied much of this lexicon of failure. The terms they used to describe people's creditworthiness – *small fry, bad egg* – entered the language. A *good-for-nothing* was someone who should not be lent anything at all, unlike someone who was 'good for a hundred dollars'. A *deadbeat* was someone it was as pointless to sue for non-payment as it would be to flog a dead horse. This new idiom, Sandage argues, turned failure into 'an imputed deficiency of self'.

In the twentieth century, according to Sandage, our definition of failure became more expansive. A failure no longer needed to be lazy or insolvent; a life lived in 'routine obscurity' was sufficient.[3] Along with the bankrupt and destitute, the 'failure' could now include the plodding time-server who never gets promoted, the dully competent middle manager or the salesman just scraping by.

Zenn Kaufman, in his 1935 book *How to Run Better Sales Contests*, approves of the new practice of companies holding competitive sales banquets for their salesmen. The salesmen would be served different courses depending on their performance measured against quotas: turkey for the top salesmen, boiled beef for the losers. Kaufman adds that their sales figures 'could also determine the size of the portion', so that 'in a friendly way both the honor and the shame are magnified'.[4] He mentions one firm which ran a sales contest dramatized as a boat race to Bermuda. The winner got the trip to Bermuda, while the lowest scorer was sent a 20lb anchor and had to pay the postage on it.

Willy Loman, in Arthur Miller's 1949 play *Death of a Salesman*, is such a failure. In any sales contest, he would be the one served boiled beef and an anchor in the mail. Loman's life is comfortable enough. Miller once said that in a kinder script he would have died on a Sunday afternoon while polishing his car. He has a loving wife and a suburban villa on which he is just about to make the last mortgage payment. It is full of 1940s mod cons – even if the fridge, vacuum cleaner and washing machine are worn out before the hire purchase payments are done. The specifics of his job don't destroy him, nor even does being fired from it. It doesn't matter what he sells: we never get to know the contents of the suitcase of samples he has been loading into his car for years. What kills him are the lies and boasts he tells himself to shore up his self-worth. Loman is an impostor, the victim of a culture that treats failure as a disease.

Miller wrote in his autobiography that in Loman he wanted to set before us 'the corpse of a believer'. By centring on someone fully signed up to the myth of success, he aimed to explode on stage 'the bullshit of capitalism, this pseudo life that thought to touch the clouds by standing on top of a refrigerator, waving a paid-up mortgage at the moon'.[5]

Miller knew how men like Loman were made. When he was fourteen, his family's successful clothing business had collapsed, a casualty of the Wall Street Crash and his father risking too much capital on the stock market's quick returns. The Millers were not ruined, quite. But they had to move from a lavish Manhattan apartment to half a small house in Brooklyn, and give up their maid, chauffeur-driven car and summer house by the beach in Queens. Family tensions over money became routine. Failure had an unseen but shattering effect on the Millers, as it did on millions of Americans.

'Attention, attention must finally be paid to such a person,' Loman's wife, Linda, says to their sons. 'And you tell me he has no character? The man who never worked a day but for your benefit? When does he get the medal for that?' The play's tragedy is that no one gets a medal for getting on with their disappointing life. An ordinary human life is now a failure until proven otherwise. No failure is wholly avoidable and no success will ever be quite enough, because both of them will always be someone else's opinion.

Loser used to be a neutral word for anyone who had suffered a loss, in sport, business or life. The *OED* dates the pejorative sense of the word – 'an unsuccessful or incompetent person, a failure' – back to only 1955. To be this kind of loser you don't need to fail in any concrete way; you just need to give off some hazy but tacitly agreed essence of loserdom. With failure, as with everything else, words matter. Sandage notes that the phrase 'I feel like a failure' is now so common that we forget it is a metaphor – 'the language of business applied to the soul'.[6]

When did the free market become the pervading aroma and undertaste of our lives? In her book *The Years*, the French writer Annie Ernaux notes how her own generation, young and radical in the 1960s, had to accommodate itself to a new reality when, in the 1980s, it reached middle age. 'Success' was suddenly the supreme value, embodied in the heroic entrepreneurs who 'started out with nothing'. The new keywords were *challenge*, *profit* and *winner*. (In English-speaking countries, the keyword was *aspirational*, with its suggestion that desiring an opulent lifestyle or a higher social station was an innately admirable trait.) The free market, Ernaux writes, assumed an 'eschatological beauty' once assigned to the utopian visions of state socialism. It stood for 'natural law, modernity, intelligence'.[7]

French historians call their study of these fluctuations in collective feeling *l'histoire de mentalités*. To a historian of mentalities, our attitudes to the world and each other are a sort of waking dream that we all dream together. When the dream changes, we change with it. Without anything being debated or decided, ideas that might once have seemed odd, or at least arguable, come to seem as normal as breathing or blinking. Our shared reality is in part a fiction built on the shifting sands of mass belief. Those who can remember when we all felt differently find themselves cut adrift, still using the old money, still dreaming a waking dream that everyone else has woken up from and replaced with another. I once saw another of Ernaux's generation, Philip Pullman, interviewed on TV, likening the bloodless victory of free market thought to being under the collective spell of a fairy-tale sorcerer.

The language of failure and success became blunter. In the 1992 film *Glengarry Glen Ross*, Chicago real-estate salesmen compete to sell worthless bits of Florida and Arizona scrubland. 'Put that coffee down,' the head-office guy, Alec Baldwin, barks at loser salesman Jack Lemmon. 'Coffee's for closers only.' Then he announces that month's sales contest: 'First prize is a Cadillac Eldorado . . . Second prize is a set of steak knives. Third prize is you're fired.'

The loser sign, with the hand raised to the forehead and the thumb and index finger extended to make the letter *L*, was a 1990s invention – as was *fail*, a one-and-a-half syllable exclamation at someone else's stupidity. This use of *fail* as a noun rather than a verb is thought to derive from the Japanese video game *Blazing Star*, which told losing players, in slightly wobbly English, 'You fail it! Your skill is not enough – See you next time – Bye-bye!' It found its way on to the web in the hashtag *epicfail*. Online, the opposite of *fail* is not success but the zero-sum *win*.

Social media is the free market untamed: a bear pit which, behind the backs of its users, provides interested parties with monetizable data about them. Its algorithms feed off snark and reward hyperbole. Its favourite words – borrowed from computer gaming or the school playground – all describe the besting of an opponent: *takedown, rinse, school, roast, burn, own* (or *self-own*, when someone tries to own someone else and it backfires). Online arguments do not shed light so much as demand winners and losers, heroes and villains. They oblige us to be always on display and held to account, one slip of the enter key from being called out and shamed. *Fake news. Virtue signaller. Pictures or it didn't happen.*

Even after she became a famous writer, Natalia Ginzburg's impostorism persisted. Her second husband, Gabriele Baldini, whom she married in 1950, was a professor of English literature at the University of Rome, and a by now familiar male figure in her life. Eloquent and assured, he loved giving her the gift of his expertise on literature, film and art. In 1960, they moved to London for two years, when Baldini became director of the Italian Cultural Institute. Accompanied everywhere by her fluent and garrulous husband, all she ever learnt to say in English was 'Have a drink?' and 'Have a cigarette?'

Ginzburg's essays often begin with confessions of intellectual laziness or ignorance about whichever subject she is discussing. When she went to the cinema, she admitted, she always lost the plot of the film and retained nothing afterwards. She had a season ticket to the opera but could never work out what was going on and so fell asleep or just sat there, 'a useless witness, lost in my own thoughts'. She talked to sociologists but felt that, compared to their lucid precision, she only 'moved in mist and emptiness'. She was a 'clueless traveller', for whom the simplest journey, or the prospect of one, meant anxiety and exhaustion.[8] We impostorists like to present ourselves like this, sincerely believing in our self-deprecation while also wearing it as an amulet to ward off failure.

The critic and novelist Oreste Del Buono was irritated by what he saw as Ginzburg's faux naivety, calling her *la finta tonta* ('the fake fool'). Another critic accused her of writing with a little girl's lisp.[9] But Ginzburg really did feel like a fool, and this recognition of her limitations may have been what saved her from despair.

One of her closest friends was the poet Cesare Pavese, with whom she worked at Einaudi and who killed himself in 1950, aged forty-one. Trying to make sense of his suicide, she decided that Pavese was unable to ascribe his errors and failures, as she did hers, to stupidity, indolence or some other human fault. He remained a prisoner of 'the bitter face and voice of reason, presenting infallible arguments to which there is no response, nothing to do but submit'.[10] He never came to terms with a recalcitrant world which disobeyed the logic of his brilliant mind. To save our lives from tragedy, Ginzburg concluded, we must accept that we cannot entirely control them. Thinking that she would fail anyway, she did not seek to bludgeon the world into making sense on her terms. She just tried to live her life day to day, imperfectly and without illusions.

A frequent theme of Ginzburg's work is what she calls 'bovarism', after the perpetually dissatisfied Madame Bovary in Flaubert's novel. In our age, she writes, 'from head to foot we are filled with bovarism, always anxious, longing, intolerant'. Secretly we believe that 'the piece of horizon we have been given is too narrow' and that 'if we had had a wider stretch of it . . . we might, perhaps, have reached a higher destiny'.[11] As the Russian saying goes: 'Life is better there where we are not.' The characters in Ginzburg's novels, like Chekhov's three sisters pining for Moscow, wait ineffectually for a better life. They have bought into the myth that there is some epicentre of success from which they have been exiled. Hope, not despair, destroys them. Rapt by a vision of the out of reach, they forget to live the life they are living.

Ginzburg never seemed to make this mistake, even as her tragedies continued. With Baldini she had two more children: Susanna, who was severely disabled, and Antonio, who died aged one. In 1969, Baldini also died, aged only forty-nine, from viral hepatitis. Through all this heartbreak, Ginzburg carried on thinking herself a failure and an impostor – but not, crucially, because she thought there was some better life just beyond reach that she could not have or did not deserve.

Italian critics have applied adjectives like *doloroso, depresivo* and *lamentoso* to Ginzburg's work. Pavese, who was one to talk, called her oeuvre *la lagna*, 'the groan'.[12] As a fellow depressive, I can't agree. I find Ginzburg's writing a solace, precisely because it refuses to sand down the world's rough edges. When sorrow is given words, however austere and unillusioned those words are, the sorrow ceases to be a formless, forbidding mass and takes on a manageable shape. By distilling life's miseries into elegant, declarative prose, Ginzburg makes them feel knowable and containable. In her writing, the beauty of form always wins out over the sadness of theme. Every one of her sentences feels like an act of quiet defiance against the cruelty of fate.

In her essay 'Summer', Ginzburg speaks to those who feel 'alienated and mortified by summer . . . judged forever unworthy of reaping the harvest of the universe'. In summer, she writes, 'we feel driven to enumerate our every grief and failing', because we cannot ever feel ourselves to be guiltlessly deserving of all the things that the season has to offer.

I too equate summer with failure. The dog days arrive as both carnival and anticlimax, proffering the world's treasures and bathing them in sunlight, but leaving my own dreams as unrealized as ever. Those days go so quickly that they remind me of my failure to live my life in the way that I keep being told I should do: smelling the mown grass, listening to the dawn chorus, living for the day. The slow death of autumn arrives as a relief. No one over-expects from the lazy sun, Arctic air and gentle rot of the fall. The slanted light and shorter days entail hunkering down and taking stock – a time for dormancy, rest and renewal. Anything we might achieve in those months is a bonus, not a demand. What a relief it is to shake off the burden of instant fulfilment and embrace life's familiar muddles and discontents.

In a 1978 paper, the clinical psychologists Pauline Clance and Suzanne Imes identified a condition they called 'the impostor phenomenon'. High-achieving women, they found, felt it most keenly. Often outnumbered by men in meetings, they were more likely to feel unentitled to be in the room. Their impostorism was self-fulfilling. The more successful they became, the more others expected of them, and the more anxious they were that they would fail to meet those expectations. The harder they worked, the more they felt that their success was only due to working harder, and the harder they had to keep working to maintain the charade.[13]

'Impostor phenomenon' is a better term than the now more common 'impostor syndrome'. A syndrome sounds like a recognized condition that can be treated but not cured – a sad, persistent fact that concerns mainly its victim and which, once it has been diagnosed, need no longer be discussed. A phenomenon sounds like something significant that demands an explanation.

For self-identifying impostors, no success will ever be enough, because no success with their name on it can have been that hard to achieve. In *Becoming*, Michelle Obama writes that in her younger life, as a high-achieving child from a mainly black, working-class part of Chicago's South Side, she turned the thrumming phrase 'not enough, not enough' over in her head 'like a malignant cell that threatened to divide and divide again'.[14] The writer George Saunders warned students at Syracuse University that 'accomplishment is unreliable' and 'success is like a mountain that keeps growing ahead of you as you hike it . . . "Succeeding" will take up your whole life, while the big questions go untended.'

Something else keeps crying 'not enough, not enough' and is like a mountain whose summit will never be reached: the free market. The free market never shuts. It reaches into every part of our lives, brooks no limits, always wants more and goes on for ever. However much wealth it gains, it never feels sated. There is always more growth to be had, a new rival to outsell, another goal to set. Corporate mission statements urge us to keep improving, to relentlessly pursue *quality*, *value* or *excellence*. And how could the quest for such elusive abstract nouns ever end?

Self-declared impostors behave exactly as the free market wants them to behave. They cannot see their success as something permanent, something they may safely deposit in a low-risk savings account where it will slowly accrue interest for ever. Instead they see it as another casino chip that they must bet away in search of a better hand, and might as easily lose. Free market capitalism is a lifelong essay crisis; it will never give them the reassurance they crave. Via smartphones and a general cult of busyness, it eats into their uncontracted hours. It delivers an infinite series of self-replenishing demands, and the only reward it offers is permission to continue the race. It is rather like that party game you played as a child where you try to eat the most cream crackers in a minute – only now the prize is that you get to eat more cream crackers.

A few years ago, the free market suffered its own very public failure. The 2008 financial crash should have woken us up with a start from our waking dream – the one where the free market acts as the thermostat that keeps our reality at its optimum temperature. It didn't. Just as in the boom-and-bust cycle of nineteenth-century America, this failure was soon forgotten. Little changed; no lessons were learnt. And then, by some casuistic sleight of hand, the blame for the crisis began to be laid elsewhere – at the door of immigrants, benefit cheats, overspending governments or rock-throwing Greeks protesting against austerity.

The risks of failure, it now became clear, had not been evenly shared. The American and European banks that almost went bust in the crash were deemed 'too big to fail' – too crucial to our economic system for their collapse to be countenanced, so that governments had to bail them out with loans and capital. The banks had already guessed that they were too big to fail, which is why they had been so reckless with other people's money. They knew they could reap the profits when their high-risk trades panned out and spread the losses when they didn't.

Before the crash, I still had a residual respect for the well-educated, articulate people, mostly white men, who ran the government, the major banks and the country. Like most sufferers from impostor syndrome, I secretly admire the charismatic confidence of those who seem immune from it. Perhaps, in some shadowy recess of my brain, I thought of these people as the natural officer class. They spoke, after all, with an unwavering poise and a bone-shuddering certainty that theirs was the only way. Surely people so dauntless must have some clue what they are doing?

The answer came soon enough: no, they did not. The crisis had been kindled by the unravelling of highly leveraged financial products, devised using mathematical models which turned out to be too complicated for actual humans to calculate the risks. These models were a story that our leaders were spinning about how the world worked. The story made scant sense, but they spun it with such conviction that they fooled even themselves.

Now I cursed my former state of innocence. I saw that the officer class had no more idea of how the world worked than I did. They were just better at covering up their ignorance with blagging and bloviation. These were the people with their hands on the tiller when the crash occurred, and, like bona fide impostors, they had been found out. But not even this unvarnished encounter with their own failings had dented their confidence or shamed them into silence. They simply carried on explaining to the rest of us how the world worked. Oh, for a tincture of their obliviousness! Having sailed the ship of state into a sandbank in broad daylight, they were now insisting that it was all the sandbank's fault. Their lunatic assurance reminded me of Monty Python's black knight, still asserting his invincibility after King Arthur has hacked off both his arms and one of his legs.

The free market never admits to its own failure, because it is a utopian project. It aims to cleanse every part of our lives with the colonic irrigation of incentivizing competition. Gone is the traditional conservatism that preferred evolution to revolution, the reliable familiar to the enticing unknown, the passable to the perfectible. In its place comes permanent revolution; the world must be remade in the shape of the free market. When this utopian project fails, the blame never lies with the project, only with the failure to realize it to the full. The free market has failed because its values have not been spread with sufficient fervour and alacrity. It feels like another version of the old Marxist line: 'Real communism has never been tried.' Failed efforts must be redoubled, so that we may continue our journey towards the utopia beyond the ever-receding horizon.

On the surface, the failing well movement appears to offer respite from this non-stop race for growth. But look more closely: there is nothing forgiving about the demand to fail well. For this demand turns failure into yet another growth opportunity, an asset that just needs to be sweated for it to become value.

Since the financial crash, the free market has embraced failure as a virtue-cum-necessity in a world without guarantees. For the new precariat, building a career means writing a CV in sand. They must do all kinds of not-quite-work – the unpaid labour of job applications and career management. They must constantly receive star ratings from customers and other instant assessments of their performance. They must be agile, adaptable, open to reskilling and refreshing their brand, shaking off rejection as if they were brushing crumbs off their clothes. We forgot to ask: why must they do this, again?

The free market wants us to think that people who work hard will be rewarded – in which case the cure for failure is to dust yourself down and start again. What can never be seen to have failed is the free market itself. The free market is the unchangeable given, so you must change instead. The failure is yours to solve, by acquiring that voguish quality that everyone now talks about: resilience.

But failure is a feature of the system, not a bug that you can eradicate by being talented and tenacious enough. All those homilies about the bracing effects of failure – they are for the little people. None of the rich and powerful people who run our lives truly believe that failure is energizing or elevating. Nor are they so naive as to own up to their own worst failures in public. They just quietly pocket their pay-offs and shelter their money where no financial crash can reach it.

Failure, like everything else in the free market, is felt unequally. You can work hard, nurture your talents lovingly and yet still fail – and your failure will be rewarded with the low status, insecurity and precarity that normally comes with failure. Or you can be an expensively schooled white man with a facile tongue, a plausible air and an unbudgeable sense of entitlement and you will be allowed to fail – endlessly, guiltlessly and ever upward.

In such a world, there is little solace to be had in learning how to fail well. You will have to find it instead in righteous anger and scorn-filled laughter. You may not be able to do anything about your failure. But you can refuse to be responsibilized into adapting to the unbending logic of a system that dispenses failure so lopsidedly. You can decide not to feel guilt or shame about failing in a world that has failed you. See? You feel better already.

Needless to say, Natalia Ginzburg was not the impostor she claimed to be. She went on to work at Einaudi for forty years. No one ever queried her lack of a degree, or asked her to leave, or otherwise found her out. Einaudi became the most prestigious publishing house in post-war Italy, and Ginzburg played her part in making the distinctive ostrich on its book spines such an imprimatur of quality. She introduced Italian readers to Ernest Hemingway, brought out the first Italian edition of Anne Frank's diary, and translated Flaubert and Maupassant. Mostly, though, she liked publishing books that others might deem commercial failures but that she was happy to share with a couple of thousand devoted readers. About her own books she shifted between feelings of resignation and shame. If she read a bad word about one of them, she would mentally disown it and tear it to shreds in her head.

'Being understood means being taken and accepted for what we are,' Ginzburg wrote. 'The saddest danger we run with other people is not so much that they don't see or don't love our qualities, but that they suppose these real qualities of ours have given birth to all kinds of other qualities which in fact are completely non-existent.'[15] Impostorism, as she knew, is not the same as low self-esteem. We self-diagnosed impostors have nothing against praise, but we would rather be undervalued than mistaken for something we are not. Consciously, we fear failure; unconsciously, we fear success and all the pretence and posturing it brings.

At the core of our neurosis lies a small seed of sanity and sense. We are searching for a world beyond success or failure, where we would not need to act like winners to disguise our fear that we are losers. We also know that the more we learn, the more confused we become. Our little landmass of knowledge looks ever smaller in the ever-expanding sea of our surrounding ignorance – but we cannot shake the feeling that this is the right way round, and that those who are not as confused as us are blessed only with a deluded clarity.

In her essay of that name, Ginzburg calls success one of 'the little virtues'. We teach our children to work hard, pass their exams and know the value of money – the little virtues we think they will need in a fallen world. The little virtues are still virtues. But on their own, without the bigger virtues to complete them, they offer 'meagre fare for human nature'. We neglect to teach our children these bigger virtues, such as generosity, courage, truthfulness and love of life, which can't be quantified and have little currency in a world impelled by the little virtues.

We teach the little virtues by threatening sanctions and

promising rewards. As soon as our children are at school we promise them money as a reward for doing well in their lessons. This is a mistake, because life itself rarely has fair rewards. Good deeds may bring no reward; bad deeds may be richly rewarded. School is a child's first encounter with this infinite universe of injustice – in which case, Ginzburg writes, our first duty is 'to console our children if they are hurt by failure'.

In a passage from 'The Little Virtues' that could be describing herself as a little girl, Ginzburg reminds us that 'sometimes a listless, solitary, bashful child is not lacking in a love of life'. The child's soul, which seems to be slumbering, is in fact 'in a state of expectancy', like 'a lizard that holds itself still and pretends to be dead but in reality it has detected the insect that is its prey and is watching its movements, and then suddenly springs forward'.[16]

Our feelings of failure often come from confusion at the life choices presented to us and fear that we have chosen badly. For Ginzburg, the universal salve for these feelings is to acquire a vocation. A vocation – from the Latin *vocare*, to call – rids us of existential anxiety by calling us to walk in one direction, sure of where we are going. In her essay 'My Vocation', Ginzburg writes that a vocation is the best way to express your love of life. It will not protect you from failure, be any kind of companion, still less offer you 'caresses and lullabies'. But it will give you a singular purpose. True satisfaction comes from giving yourself over each day to your vocation. Whether you succeed or fail at it, you will be living your own life.

Writing, for Ginzburg, was not a way of amassing achievements but a way of belonging to the world. Because she had a vocation, it did not matter that she thought herself 'a small, a very small writer'. It was enough to know that no one wrote exactly like her, 'however much a mosquito or a flea of a writer I may be'.[17] With a vocation, you can't feel like an impostor, because your life is about the work, not you. Any success – which, in an iniquitous world, will always be unreliable – comes as a fortuitous side effect of your calling.

I once watched a carpenter build a handrail for the stairs near my office at work. It took him three days. I passed and nodded to him several times each day, as he lovingly turned a long block of pine into a curved, grooved pole shaped for the human hand. Then he sanded it down and varnished it until it was smooth as laminate. Then he made little pencil marks on the wall above the stairs, drilled holes for the bracket screws and mounted the rail very tenderly as if it were a work of art on a gallery wall. This ordinary object came to seem beautiful in light of the patient effort it took him to make it. Once it was up, he left without waiting for praise or thanks, leaving an everyday object that everyone noticed once and then forgot was even there. That carpenter had no need of our approval; he had a vocation.

If you feel like a failure, or an impostor, or both, you will find in Natalia Ginzburg a fast and firm friend. As friends are supposed to do, she will make you feel less weird and less alone. For all her insecurities, her fortitude in the face of loss will steady you. For all her loathing of false consolations, her truth-seeking will console you. And for all her self-confessed timidity, her calm, clear voice will give you the courage to breathe in your worst failures, slowly exhale, and carry on with your bullet-holed but still beautiful life.

3.

The Examination Dream

Or how we are schooled to feel like failures

Every few months or so, I dream the examination dream.

In this dream, I must resit a school exam in midlife. I keep being stopped from revising for it by inane interruptions from family and friends. They cannot be made to see that, although I am no longer a student, I have an exam to sit. Trapped inside the unstoppable logic of a dream, I never question my need to sit it, even though I know I passed the same exam years ago, so I have nothing to gain and much to lose by sitting it again.

I arrive at the exam hall and am embarrassed to find myself seated alongside much younger candidates, even younger than the students I teach. As the papers are handed out, my state of barely contained panic contrasts with the composure of everyone else in the hall. Then I turn over the paper and discover that I am in the wrong exam, or the set texts are not the ones I have prepared, or the pages are blank.

Then I wake up. It takes a few seconds of post-slumber muzziness for me to clock where I am. My breathing slows as the relief kicks in. I no longer have to sit an exam for which I am woefully unprepared, and come the dawn I may return to the everyday, middle-aged agitations for which I am woefully unprepared.

In *The Interpretation of Dreams*, Sigmund Freud notes how common the examination dream is and what a strikingly similar form it takes whoever is dreaming it. 'It is in vain that they object,' he writes of these examination dreamers, 'even while they are still asleep, that for years they have been practising medicine or working as University lecturers or heads of offices.'

Freud never quite decided why people dreamt this dream. His first theory was that their unconscious was punishing them for their self-perceived failures. As children, our wrongdoings are promptly and explicitly punished by our elders. As adults, we no longer hear such simplifying verdicts. To hear them again we must return to the exam hall, where judgement is decisive and failure categorical.

But then a colleague of Freud pointed out that only those who had been successful at exams ever dreamt the examination dream. Freud had failed forensic medicine in his university finals but never dreamt about that. Instead his unconscious kept making him resit exams in botany, zoology and chemistry that he had passed with distinction.

So Freud devised a second theory, that the examination dream offered solace. It occurred when the dreamer had some stressful task ahead of them and was afraid it would be a fiasco. By revisiting a tense but successfully surmounted chapter in the dreamer's youth, this dream was telling the dreamer: 'Don't be afraid of tomorrow! Just think how anxious you were before your Matriculation, and yet nothing happened to you. You're a doctor, etc., already.'[1] That theory makes some sense to me, because I was good at exams and did not find them traumatic – at least, no more traumatic than I found life in general.

I have another theory, though, one that Freud never considered. I dream the examination dream because I unconsciously wish that I'd failed my exams, since their judgement of me as competent and well informed was, if not quite a sham, then a simplification. Part of me feels that it was all too easy, that the entire pantomime was assessing an arbitrary set of skills – good memory, strong nerves, capacity for coming out with plausible bullshit against the clock – at which I happened arbitrarily to excel. The dream is yet another symptom of my impostor syndrome. My unconscious, allowed free rein in deep sleep, is telling me that I did not deserve to pass my exams for such trivial reasons, and so I will have to sit them again and again in my dreams for ever.

Examinations began in the early seventh century, in Sui dynasty China, as a way of selecting the brightest young men for civil service. By 1644, at the start of the last imperial dynasty, Qing, China had a vast system of exams. Each succeeding dynasty had used these exams to strengthen the emperor's power. Exam procedures and paperwork spread his influence into every part of his sprawling empire. It meant that anyone in any important position owed that position to him. Lower down the food chain, the hundreds of thousands of exam candidates gave little thought to sedition or rebellion. They were too busy revising.

Imagine a young Chinese exam candidate, circa 1650. We must begin in the womb, for even before a Chinese boy is born his family have begun dreaming of his examination success and the honour it will bring to the family. (Girls can't sit exams and incur dowries, so a man with only daughters is said to be childless.) A pregnant woman, to improve the exam prospects of her unborn child, avoids harsh colours and listens to poetry read aloud. When a boy is born, she celebrates by scattering coins for her servants inscribed with the legend 'first-place graduate'.

When her boy is three, she starts to tutor him, using a Confucian primer. Thus begins his long mission of regurgitating verbatim the Four Books and Five Classics, works attributed to Confucius or his disciples. At the village school, his hours are filled with learning by rote. At intervals he is called up to the teacher's desk to recite by heart a few lines from Confucius. If he gets them right, he may begin work on the next few lines. If he falters on a single word, he is thwacked on the palms and thighs with a fan-shaped ruler and sent back to his desk to start again. He spends his teenage years sitting licensing and qualifying exams at county, department and prefecture level. A bright boy, he passes them all. He is now a first-degree graduate, *xiucai*, or 'budding talent'.

At the age of twenty, he travels with his family to Nanjing for the provincial examination, held every three years in September, a week before the harvest moon. He arrives on horseback, carrying a banner that identifies him as a candidate, and a large basket. The basket contains his inkstick, inkstone, writing brush, writing paper (for rough), writing silk (for best), candles, bedding, a water pitcher, a portable furnace and some rice and dumplings in a pot.

The Jiangnan Examination Hall is like a prison, enclosed by a wall of thorns. To enter it, he must submit to a brutal body search. The guards are looking for cheat-sheets wrapped in his bedding, or cheating shirts, inner gowns with the Confucian classics written on them in minuscule print. The examination will last three days, during which time they seal the latch bar on the Great Gate and no one may enter or leave. If a candidate gets sick, or dies, the guards will wrap his body in straw matting and throw it over the wall. Not even death stops an examination.

Inside the compound, our candidate is allocated one of thousands of tiny cells, no bigger than a stationery cupboard and consisting of bare brick walls, a roof and a floor of impacted dirt. Each cell is open on one side and surveyed by guards in watchtowers. Two wooden boards must serve as his seat, desk and bed.

He reads the set essay topic: 'He who delights in Heaven will affect with his love and protection the whole Empire.' He must answer using a strict form known as the eight-legged essay, with its eight never-to-be-deviated-from parts, from *poti* (break open the topic) to *dajie* (conclude the topic). Over the next three days, he heaves out all his learning in his best calligraphic hand. When he gets hungry, he cooks his rice and dumplings on his little furnace. When he gets tired, he tries to sleep a little, although the cell is so cramped he can't extend his legs fully and the sight of candles alight in other cells makes him feel guilty for resting.

At last a cannon sounds to signal the exam's end. He trudges out of the compound while, like millions of exam candidates before and since, cursing the perversity of the examiners and convincing himself that he has failed. He rejoins his family, who have been waiting outside the whole time, along with thousands of others. It takes days for the essays to be marked. Then, unannounced, officials bring out a placard on which they write the names of the successful candidates in sequence, from the sixth man down. Hope drains from his heart as the list gets longer, all the way down to the bottom, and his name fails to appear. But then they write the top five names. He has come first! He is now a *juren*, an 'elevated man', with a job as an official for life.

Yet the long climb to the imperial heights continues. The following spring, he sits a final exam in the Imperial Palace in Beijing. In the Hall of Preserving Harmony, he turns over the exam paper and reads an address from the chief examiner: the emperor himself. 'I am the Son of Heaven, responsible for governing the Empire,' it begins. 'Night and day I rack My brains so that the people will be able to live in tranquillity. Fortunately I have this opportunity to pose questions to you graduates and I wish to hear your well-considered opinions on the following.' The candidate begins his essay as if answering the emperor: 'Your humble servant replies to Your question; Your humble servant has heard.'

A few days later, the list of names of those who have passed is written on a golden placard, laid in a sedan chair, paraded through the city and set down by the East Chang'an Gate. Once again his name appears at the top. He is the *optimus*: the number-one scholar, one of the 'stars in heaven' who will stand at the emperor's right hand, advising him on how to bring harmony to the empire. That night he attends a celebratory banquet. He receives a decorated hat, a sceptre and eighty ounces of silver to build a triumphal arch at his home. When he finally arrives back in his little village, his friends hold him aloft on their shoulders and his tearful family enfold him in their arms.

From the mid sixteenth century onwards, European missionaries and diplomats visited China and commended its exam system. Jesuit missionary Matteo Ricci praised China as a land ruled by scholar-gentlemen, Plato's dream of an aristocracy of talent made real. The Jesuits adopted written exams for their schools and for admission to their order. Voltaire, who never visited China, thought it a kind of utopia. 'The human mind certainly cannot imagine a government better than this one,' he wrote, 'where everything is to be decided by the large tribunals, subordinated to each other, of which the members are received only after several severe examinations.'

In the nineteenth century, the written exam gradually became the norm all over Europe. The 1854 Northcote–Trevelyan Report recommended competitive examinations for entry to the British civil service, along the Chinese model. Four years later, the first public exams for English schools, administered by Oxford and Cambridge universities, took place.

Michael Young's work of imaginary history, *The Rise of the Meritocracy*, begins here. The book's narrator is a government sociologist, writing in the year 2034. His theme is the transformation of Britain, over the previous century and three-quarters, into a complete meritocracy. Until the Northcote–Trevelyan Report, he argues, British society had been governed by nepotism and patronage, and all social classes had 'their fair share of geniuses and morons'.[2] But such feudalism had put a brake on efficiency and Britain feared it would be overtaken economically by other nations. So education was made compulsory and the school exam system began.

A counter-voice in Young's story is R. H. Tawney, the socialist historian who remained quaintly attached to egalitarianism as meritocracy took hold. In his 1931 book *Equality*, Tawney argued for a more equal society, not simply one organized by that newly touted ideal, equality of opportunity. Only actual equality, he felt, would truly spread opportunities, for equality 'depends, not only upon an open road, but upon an equal start'.[3] But in Young's narrative (and in real life), Tawney lost the argument to Fabian socialists like H. G. Wells and George Bernard Shaw. Their dream was of an intellectual samurai, an elite of experts to steer enlightened social reform. They believed in something that did not yet have a name: meritocracy.

A key event in Young's narrator's story is the 1944 Education Act, which made secondary education both free and selective. Then, in the 1960s and 1970s (which is where Young's book, published in 1958, becomes a work of prophetic fiction), the meritocrats won a vital battle against the new threat of comprehensive schools, successfully arguing that their sentimental egalitarianism bred only mediocrity. Soon the grammar schools were so well funded that they outclassed the private schools. The best private schools became boarding grammars; the worst became finishing schools for the dim-witted offspring of the rich. In the new psychometric science, the IQ of a foetus could be reliably foretold. The country was at last ruled by 'the five per cent of the nation who know what five per cent means'.[4]

But now, in 2034, this meritocratic Eden has a canker at its heart. The rich and powerful have lost all sympathy for the people below them and feel that their own success is only their just deserts. The poor and powerless, meanwhile, have no excuse for their lowly state. Robots have replaced them in the factories and those not unemployed are working as domestic servants. Inequality of opportunity had at least let them hold on to the reassuring myth of human equality. Now, tested to the hilt and labelled dunces, they are angry and without hope.

As the narrator's story draws to a close, his meritocratic utopia lies in peril. A mob has ransacked the Ministry of Education and a general strike has been called, with a demonstration on May Day. The narrator is unperturbed, believing that, emptied of all intellect and ability, the lower classes are now a mere rabble. A final footnote at the end of the book informs us that he was killed in the May uprising, before he even got to check the proofs of the book we have just read.

Young's narrator sounds sweetly reasonable, just as meritocracy sounds like a sweetly reasonable idea. It seems obvious that ability and application should be rewarded and that the most gifted people should be in charge. And yet Young's meritocracy deserves to fall. It is a heartless realm where human beings have become little more than implements of competitive efficiency, and education, like Victorian charity, is denied to the undeserving poor. The House of Commons has handed power to the civil service and a House of Lords stuffed with clever life peers. In this perfect meritocracy, democracy is dead.

In the mid twentieth century, when Young wrote his book, Britain's meritocracy was incomplete. Back then, as his narrator says, 'it was still not unknown for King's or Balliol to detect some special merit in sons whose fathers had been there before'.[5] This was the world in which Alan Bennett, a butcher's son from Leeds, took the Oxford University entrance exam in 1954 and won a scholarship. When he sat his history finals three years later, he got a first-class degree that surprised everyone, not least himself. Half a century later, he wrote an essay in which he confessed that he had cheated in all these exams.

Not many would call it cheating. All Bennett did, in the lead-up to the exams, was dice arguments and quotations into 'minced morsels' that fitted on a batch of correspondence cards he carried everywhere, a sort of portable exam-prep kit. Then he looked at lots of old exam papers and practised turning each question into a formula that could use whatever was on his cards. He had also sussed that answering an exam question was a bit like journalism, that 'going for the wrong end of the stick was more attention-grabbing'.[6] In 1957, he saw all this as cheating – and more than half a lifetime later, he still did.

Bennett's play *The History Boys* follows eight boys at a Sheffield grammar school in the 1980s being tutored for Oxbridge. One of their teachers is Hector, a traditionalist who champions learning for its own sake and thinks exams the enemy of education, a 'Cheat's Visa'. The other is Irwin, newly hired by the headmaster to school the boys in exam technique, in the hope that Oxbridge places will bring his school glory and a hike up the league tables. Irwin's method is to liven up the boys' essays so they stand out in the piles of papers that admissions tutors read. He teaches them how to grab a tutor's attention with odd facts, killer quotes and contrarian arguments. Irwin thinks that 'truth is no more at issue in an examination than thirst at a wine-tasting or fashion at a striptease'.

Like Irwin, the young Bennett realized that the Oxford examiners prized slantwise thinking and verbal flourish. Exams were essentially ludic, a sort of scholarly swordsmanship, a licensed showing-off. Hence they demanded a costume: the subfusc of charcoal suit, black shoes, white shirt, bow tie, mortarboard and gown that he had to wear in the exam hall.

This aspect of Oxford's exams had its roots in the Middle Ages. Medieval university examinations involved not silent scribbling at desks but viva voces modelled on the rituals of courts of law or the athletics trials of antiquity. The disputation, in which the candidate affirmed a thesis and an opponent refuted it, owed much to the pseudo-combat of the medieval joust. From the end of the eighteenth century, Oxford moved gradually to written exams. But the exams remained coloured by these associations with sport and combat. They prized quick thought, conspicuous erudition and rhetorical flair – intellectual life as a competitive game.

One Oxford exam today retains this sense of scholarly theatre. Anyone with a first in their finals is invited to sit the All Souls Prize Fellowship Examination – a gruelling two-day rite in early autumn, with four papers of three hours each. The essay questions are purposely left-field, aimed at testing mental nimbleness and native wit. *What is a person? Why is a leather jacket more acceptable than a fur coat? Can we be forced to be free? Do you own your own body? Would you rather be a vampire or a zombie? Are there too many books? Does Google know us better than we do? Are there any serious works about dragons? If not, write one.* Most candidates, thus far the brightest stars in the exam firmament, fail to dazzle enough.

In imperial China, the examination graduate was one bright star amid tens of thousands of failures. Sons of peasants, traders or artisans couldn't even afford to sit the exams. It all required money – for tutors, books, writing materials, travel, lodgings, tips for officials and thank-you gifts (or bribes) for examiners. And no man could sit an exam if anyone in his family, in the last three generations, had engaged in a 'base occupation' such as running a brothel or being an actor.

For those allowed to sit the exams, the years of toil usually came to nothing. If a candidate slightly misquoted Confucius – even a single false stroke on a single character – he failed. If his candle fell and burned a hole in his writing silk, or if he stained it with wax, or if he smudged a single letter of his calligraphy by letting a lone raindrop fall on it, or if he carelessly skipped a page in the answer book, or if he strayed even slightly from the eight legs of the eight-legged essay, or if an examiner (given just a few days to wade through stacks of scripts all numbered to preserve anonymity) got his brilliant answer mixed up with a dud, then he failed.

His failure had only two possible causes: fate (*ming*) and luck (*fu*). Either the gods had preordained his poor ranking or he had run out of the finite sum of good fortune with which every man is born. This did little to thin the ranks of fortune tellers, geomancers and I Ching diviners to whom mothers went looking for hints of their son's future success, nor the army of mediums who claimed to spirit-write the quotes from Confucius that would be on the exam.

Most candidates never got beyond the local examinations. At these exams, uncapped youths – those yet to go through the coming-of-age capping ceremony that marked a boy's fifteenth year – were given easier questions and marked leniently. So every candidate pretended to be fourteen, including career exam-sitters deep into middle age. The invigilators gazed pityingly on their lined foreheads, greying temples, receding hairlines and stubbly chins pitted with razor cuts – and turned a blind eye.

The exam system produced legions of learned men, over-educated and permanently stung by disappointment. Between the ages of seventeen and fifty-six, the Shandong writer An Zhiyuan (1628–1701) sat and failed the provincial examination fifteen times in a row. On his seventieth birthday, he looked back on his part in the 'battle of letters'. He wondered at the wearying journeys west he had made to his provincial capital, Jinan, on a donkey, quivering in his student's gown in the early autumn chill. 'When I recalled the ancient saying, "Failure and success are governed by fate," I felt as though I had awakened from a dream or recovered from a drunken stupor,' he wrote. 'I can only grieve that in the twilight of my life I cannot halt the passage of time.'

An remembered how, in the spring of 1666, he had climbed the sacred mountain, Taishan. Halfway up, he met a white-haired Taoist who looked hard at him and said: 'You are not destined to be eminent in the realm of dust. Come and meet me here beneath the tall pine tree in ten years' time, and I will speak with you of things outside this world.' An, not yet forty and still dreaming of examination glory, ignored the old man's offer. Now, many failures later, he lamented that 'the Taoist immortal has gone I know not where'.[7]

Another Shandong writer, Pu Songling (1640–1715), had, aged eighteen, passed top of the class in his local exams. Two years later, he failed the provincial exam – then carried on failing it for the rest of his life, while scraping a living as a private tutor. In 1679, as his fortieth birthday approached, he chided himself for wasting his life on useless study: 'I drink to propel my pen, but succeed only in venting my spleen, my lonely anguish.'

Pu's collection of stories *Strange Tales from a Chinese Studio* is full of eternal students, their lives forever clouded by an impending exam. When they fail, they 'cry in torment, wishing they were dead, but in the eyes of a spectator there is no sight more ludicrous'. Some characters die and their ghosts sit the exams for them. One scholar returns to his village in jubilation as a *juren*, only to be told by his wife that he has been dead for three years and they still can't afford a proper burial.

In Pu's story 'The Seven Likenesses of a Candidate', a provincial exam candidate is likened to seven things. When entering the exam compound, bare-footed and panting under his basket's load and shouted at by guards, he is 'like a prisoner'. When writing in his cell and stretching his neck to peer out at the other inmates, he is 'like a cold bee late in autumn'. When leaving the compound, his brain spent and his legs buckling, he is 'like a sick bird let out of a cage'. When awaiting the results, dreaming of the great mansions he might live in but still fearing failure, he is 'like a monkey on a leash'. When he finds out that he has failed, he is 'like a poisoned fly no longer able to move'. When he wails at the unfairness of exams, sets his books on fire, stamps on the ashes, throws them in the gutter and resolves to head for the mountains, he is like 'a pigeon smashing its own precious eggs'. When his anger abates, he starts all over again 'like a turtle dove just hatched'.

Pu was ever that turtle dove, rebuilding his nest and resolving to try just one more time. According to a sketch of his wife that he wrote shortly after her death in 1713, when he reached his fifties she had pleaded with him to give up. She pointed out that if he were meant to be important he would be a minister by now. 'One can find happiness here among the hills and woods,' she said. 'Why need you look for entertainments in the music of bamboo striking flesh?' Pu conceded that this was good counsel, but that when he saw his grandson going off to take the provincial exam his old hopes stirred. 'I have no other virtues,' his wife told him, 'but I do know where to stop.'[8] Pu at last gave up sitting exams a year after his wife died. He was seventy-two.

Somewhere on this earth, whatever the time of year, young people are enduring what in Japan they call *shiken jigoku*: examination hell.

Around ten million young Chinese sit the high school leaving exam, *gaokao*, each year. Their whole school career leads up to it. *Gaokao* stragglers are sent to 'exam towns', mega high schools where they sleep in dorms, with their families in rented rooms nearby. The classrooms have digital displays, counting down the days to *gaokao*. The teachers speak through headset mics to keep the students awake.

A Chinese saying compares *gaokao* to 'a stampede of thousands of soldiers and tens of thousands of horses across a single log bridge'. As the sole criterion for admission into Chinese universities, a student's three-figure *gaokao* score is the ineluctable verdict on their young life. Universities rank in strict and unyielding order, with the Beijing ones, Peking and Tsinghua, at the top. Teachers instil in their students the ultimate fear – that if they fail they will have to attend a third-tier university. During Mao's Cultural Revolution, the *gaokao* was abolished and the rural poor were idealized. Now hardly any young Chinese want to live in the country. *Gaokao* success converts into a place at a top university, then a good job in a big city. Two in five students fail to get into any university at all.

On 7 June, the two-day, nine-hour ritual of *gaokao* begins. Police cars turn off their sirens and drivers are banned from honking their horns. Noisy factories and building sites shut down. The square dancers who perform to music in public squares switch off their amplifiers. Extra police patrol to ensure that *gaokao* sitters can find their way to the exam halls. Ticket inspectors wave them through metro stations and taxi drivers give them free rides. Their parents go to Confucian temples to light lanterns and pray.

At the allotted hour, all around the world, the ritual plays out the same. A mass of young bodies is decanted into a school hall or gymnasium. They walk in on the unnerving but geometrically appealing sight of hundreds of desks arranged singly and in symmetrical rows. They each settle at a numbered desk, laying out their pencil cases (see-through, to prevent cheating), bottles of water (with the label taken off) and tissues (exams often coinciding with high pollen counts). Over the next few hours, these desks, spaced a regulation distance apart, will become little islands of anxious industry. Each island's lone inhabitant will write the story of their future, while wondering what will happen if they fail.

For those few hours each islander will feel entirely alone. But they may also feel a peculiar intimacy with the islanders around them, the backs of whose heads they will get to know well. These are their exam peers, to whom they are linked by two simple facts: their mothers gave birth in the same school year and their surnames meet in the alphabet. Perhaps they even feel linked to the desk-inhabiting islanders in other school gyms across the country – perfect strangers who are also being asked, at this very moment, about oxbow lakes, or the reactivity of halogens, or the square root of 64.

None of them would choose to be here, islanded on a desk in

a wide gymnasium sea. Neither did they choose to spend all those hours in box bedrooms, kept awake by caffeine and adrenaline, amending over-optimistic revision timetables, drawing mnemonic mind maps and colouring their notes with fluorescent highlighters. They have fretted and moaned about it all for months, and the fretting and moaning have spread among them through cross-infection. But few question why they have to go through it. For that would be to question their own culture's main criteria for success – and that would mean silencing the background hum of social habit and cultural meaning that makes them feel at home in the world.

The second hand of the wall clock ticks noisily up to the hour and the signal is given: 'You may begin.' The sound of mass fluttering attends the turning over of papers. Now they become the 'dull blear-eyed scribbling fools' whom Rupert Brooke mocks and pities in his poem 'In Examination'. They write until their wrists and palms ache, exams being the last citadel of handwriting in this age of the hypertrophied texting thumb.

Silence, gravid with nervous energy, fills the room. Only the occasional echoing cough, or the subdued creak of a polypropylene chair, or an invigilator's heels click-clacking on the parquet floor, intrudes. Every so often an arm goes up, its owner wanting more paper or to go to the toilet. Then the clock's minute hand reaches the vertical for the final time. The chief invigilator tells the room to stop writing, as if she is passing sentence. Downed pens rattle on desks. Muted sighs and stifled laughs accompany the collecting of the papers. Only when the chief invigilator is happy that the number of scripts corresponds with the number of bodies sat at desks are those bodies allowed to leave. With a cacophonous scraping of chairs, they are set free like caged birds into the daylight and air, squealing with relief.

In Britain, results day comes one Thursday in August. Local newspaper photographers are despatched to school playgrounds to take pictures of successful students celebrating by leaping in the air. Those who have failed are allowed to weep off camera. Over on social media, celebrities list the poor grades they got years earlier, with a version of this message: 'Don't worry about your results: look how badly I did!' (Implied coda: 'And look at me now!') This new and perhaps kindly-meant custom is a recipe for cognitive confusion. At the very moment young people are forced to confront official and unambiguous failure, and after being warned for years by their teachers what that failure might mean, they are told that they have no right to be sad.

The most anxious person come results day is neither a student nor a parent. It is the secondary school head teacher, who sleeps and eats fitfully in the weeks leading up to that fateful Thursday in late summer. What will the governors, the parents and the local press think if the school's results are bad and its league-table ranking slips? These rankings, meant to foster competition between schools and drive up standards, are never far from a head teacher's thoughts. They also inform the inspections carried out by Ofsted, the Office for Standards in Education. Among teachers, the name Ofsted stirs a primitive dread. Ofsted can label schools as 'failing'. Failing schools face the shame of greater scrutiny, takeover by successful schools, even closure. When students fail, their schools and their teachers fail too.

Every year sees the same public bloodletting over the results, the same unwinnable arguments about standards. People complain all over again that the exams have got too easy or been marked too softly. Behind these arguments lies a shibboleth: exams are a gold standard. A C grade in maths must have a fixed value, like the square root of 64, that stays the same for ever. And it must have a fixed equivalence with a C grade in a completely different subject, such as English or Latin.

The bothersome truth is that not everything can be so easily counted and computed, because we can't simply step outside our own untidy human judgements. Few want to admit this. It is as if we are collectively riding a symbolic bicycle, and if we thought too much about working the pedals and keeping our balance, we would fall off. Falling off a bicycle is painful and it makes us look foolish. So we keep the faith instead.

In imperial China, keeping the examination faith was the work of a lifetime. The long-nourished dream of being a star of heaven haunts the characters in Wu Ching-tzu's classic novel *The Scholars* (*c.*1750). Of those few that achieve it, none feel lifted into earthly paradise. Their only reward is the emptiness that comes from satisfying ambitions that are not quite their own.

Chou Chin, already over sixty when we meet him first in the novel, keeps failing his local examinations and has to eke out a living as a teacher and accountant. By now he is so traumatized by failure that when he sets foot in a provincial examination cell he gives out a sigh, dashes his head against the wooden boards, blacks out and falls to the ground. Nevertheless, he sits the exam and not only passes but, amazingly, comes first.

The villagers who had Chou Chin dismissed from his post as a teacher now build a shrine, its centrepiece a memorial tablet on which appears in gold letters an account of his brilliant career. Scrolls of his calligraphy are taken down from the wall, sprinkled with water to preserve them and remounted as holy relics. Strangers claim him as a friend.

Another of Wu's characters, Fan Chin, keeps failing the provincial exam and, at fifty-four, has sunk his family into ruin. His father-in-law, a butcher named Hu, mocks Fan Chin's threadbare clothes and calls him a scarecrow. Fan Chin asks Hu for money to make one last journey to the provincial exam. 'Don't be a fool!' Hu replies, spitting in his face. 'You're like a toad trying to swallow a swan! You should piss on the ground and look at your face in the puddle! You look like a monkey, yet you want to become an official.'

Fan Chin scrabbles the money together anyway and goes to

the provincial capital to take the exam. On his return, he learns that his family has gone without food for two days and he must go to the market and sell their last laying hen just to buy a few portions of rice to make gruel. While at the market, Fan Chin hears that three heralds on horseback have arrived at his home. He has come seventh on the examination list. He runs wildly around town screaming 'I passed!' and carries on screaming even after falling into a slime-filled pond. The townspeople flock to Fan Chin's home, offering money, rice, land, servants, silver chopsticks and fine porcelain. Butcher Hu now claims to have always thought his son-in-law learned and fine-looking, and to have turned down rich suitors because he knew his daughter would marry an important man.

Fan Chin is made commissioner of education for Shandong Province. But then he disgraces himself. In conversation with other scholars, he reveals his ignorance of one of China's greatest poets, Su Shi. Like all the other prize scholars, Fan Chin's knowledge is shallow; he has never bothered to read beyond the few Confucian classics that appear on the exam. 'Even Confucius,' says another student, 'if he were alive today, would be studying essays and preparing for the examinations instead of saying "Make few false statements and do little you may regret."' Why? Because that kind of talk would get him nowhere: nobody would give him an official position.' The scholars have learnt only to turn the moral authority of Confucius into examiner-satisfying sanctimony. They no longer even glance at those classics that they picked up as a battering ram to open the door to honour and eminence, then threw aside as soon as the door gave way.

The scholars believed that their empty lives would be miraculously transformed by passing exams. As the proverb says: 'There are golden mansions in study; there are bushels of rice and beautiful women.' Those that pass do feel as if transported to heaven – but the joy lasts barely as long as the sound of the heralds announcing their triumph. They have replaced their rags with crimson robes and gilded belts, and the lowly candidates they once were now bow before them. But their success has not freed them from themselves. The only free people in Wu's novel are the true scholars who go off to the mountains to live as hermits, trying to anchor their lives in something more than this crazed clamber up the examination mountain to become a star of heaven.

One of these truly free people may have been Wu Ching-tzu himself. He was born into a prominent family in which the men had held high office for generations. As a youth, he was good at exams. Then his father offended his elders for some obscure reason and lost his job as an official, dying a year later, when Wu was twenty-three. His father's downfall disillusioned Wu and he began to squander his inheritance. Aged twenty-eight, he scandalized his community by sitting the local licensing examination while drunk. Aged thirty-three, he moved to Nanjing, where he spent his time partying. Until his death at fifty-three he lived, in near penury, off small sums of money from his writing.

Living inside a culture, we so invest in its rituals that we fail to see them as rituals at all. Human life only looks strange to us when seen from the distance of time and space. How odd the exam rituals of Qing dynasty China appear, how cruel the rigours of *gaokao*, compared to our own more sensible and logical arrangements! The success markers of faraway lands seem so arbitrary, the effort expended to win them so stupidly disproportionate. Our own rituals, caked in layers of custom and confirmation bias, are safe from our scorn. We fail to see how they have seduced us and blinded us to other ways of ordering the world. The behavioural scientist Paul Dolan calls them 'narrative traps': tales we tell ourselves about how we ought to live our lives, which end up making us sad.

The Earl of Rochester called a human being 'that vain animal / Who is so proud of being rational'. The stories that make us most sad are the ones we have hidden beneath a veneer of scientificity – like the one that tells us that talent can be neatly subdivided and measured and that we can find a fair way of rewarding people based on this measure.

Every society rewards the human qualities it has chosen to value. Universities are now viewed mainly as engines of economic growth. The government's definition of a successful university course is one where the size of its tuition fees correlates with the size of salary a graduate of that course can command. Measurable inputs need to match measurable outputs. We tell students, in so many words, that to be successful they must be a human resource, a package of skills to sell on. The traditional aims of a humane education – to help young people find meaning in their lives and to develop their gifts in a way that is true to themselves and useful to others – have come to seem naive and retrograde.

In a meritocracy, your worth as human capital is what counts. Extracting maximum value from that capital means not consulting too closely your own passions. It leaves less time for the kind of free-ranging curiosity that might help to answer the questions that all young people want answering: Who am I? What am I doing here? How can I best live my life? Worse than failure, perhaps, is feeling trapped inside a cycle of overachievement in pursuit of a success that at heart you don't believe in.

This is meritocracy's fatal flaw: not that it sets up people to fail but that it defines so meanly what success means. In focusing on quasi-objective targets we have already set, it ignores the human potential we can't yet measure. It asks people to play a game they did not ask to play, with the rules set by someone else, for a prize they may not want. This too can feel like failure.

Before the word *meritocracy* even existed, R. H. Tawney coined a phrase, 'the tadpole philosophy'. This philosophy, Tawney argued, was how an unequal society justified itself – by convincing all the tadpoles that they might shake off their failed lives and get to be frogs. Each of the tadpoles, he wrote, tells itself it will be one of the tiny number that 'will one day shed their tails, distend their mouths and stomachs, hop nimbly on to dry land, and croak addresses to their former friends on the virtues by means of which tadpoles of character and capacity can rise to be frogs'.[9]

What the tadpoles can't see is that they don't really fail or succeed at all. Their metamorphosis has little to do with effort or merit. Hormonal changes, not hard work and talent, make their gills shrink away and their frog limbs grow. All a tadpole need do, to finish its twelve-week course and graduate as a froglet, is find enough to eat and avoid being eaten itself by the diving beetles, water scorpions and dragonfly larvae that gobble most of its tadpole peers up.

But what's so wrong with being a tadpole? Every tadpole has already graduated with honours from frogspawn. Once upon a time it was just a black dot trapped inside jelly. Then one end of the dot grew a head, and the other a tail, and it forced its way out. (Most of the other black dots weren't so lucky.) A tadpole has a right to its blameless, vegetarian, tadpoley life, the same right to be on this earth as any other living thing. That life may be brief and cosmically insignificant, but so, in the deep time of the universe, is the life of a frog, or a human. We tend to extol the virtues of lungs and legs over the feathery gills and finned tails of tadpoles. But we would do, wouldn't we? We have lungs and legs.

Michael Young wrote *The Rise of the Meritocracy* as a warning. Long before he died, in 2002, the word *meritocracy* had shed all these dystopian associations. Instead, and much to his chagrin, it had become the solve-all for an unfair world, the gallant slayer of privilege, the promise of social mobility to sugar the pill of inequality. In its name had arrived a culture of constant testing, measurement and ranking. Young's satire might now even be misread as a bible for this new religion.

Young believed that having one definition of merit, trying to sieve everyone through the same narrow mesh into a bowl of measurable worth, would induce doubt and despair in those that didn't make it through. He did not foresee that it might also induce doubt and despair in those that did. His fictional meritocrats are all smugly convinced of their superiority. Such people do exist in real life, of course. That is how meritocracy works, explaining away privilege with self-flattering notions of merit. But not everyone succumbs so easily to flattery. A war's victors can still be miserable if they never chose to fight it in the first place.

Anyone who teaches young people will have spotted the symptoms of an invisible epidemic of anxiety. I have had students slumped in front of me in my office, so sunk in unreachable misery that I have been clueless as to how to help. Not that all, or even most of them, suffer like this – just enough of them to make us wonder what on earth is going on, even if we can't know the roots of their misery, for misery's roots have many branches.

When distressed students receive help, it comes mainly in the form of advice about living well. They are offered mindfulness training, or sessions with therapy dogs, or guidance about healthy eating and sleeping well. All these things may help. But they are blister plasters applied to a gaping wound – and, what's more, plasters that the patient has to self-administer. That new boilerplate phrase 'mental health and wellbeing' sounds to me as if it is trying to turn fierce emotional pain into something blandly managerial. Social pathologies can't be repaired with life hacks and self-care.

The radical therapist David Smail used the term 'magical voluntarism' to describe this fallacy that we can stop a dysfunctional world causing us distress purely through our own efforts. In magical voluntarism, the miserable must acclimatize themselves to the system that is making them miserable. All that happens is they become more depressed. Depression is an internalized protest, a silent remonstration against reality. Instead of getting usefully angry with the way the world works, your mind berates itself. As success recedes further from your reach, you tell yourself that you just have to shake off your failure and try harder. Cruel optimism, indeed.

The exam system is sometimes compared to a forcing house – like those darkened sheds in Yorkshire's rhubarb triangle, where the rhubarb grows so rapidly that you can hear it squeak and pop. But that metaphor doesn't really work. In a forcing house, growth may be artificially enhanced but at least things grow. Forced rhubarb is not quite as nature intended, but it still tastes deliciously sour-sweet.

A better metaphor for the exam system, I think, is a well-tended lawn. A lawn is a monoculture. It swaps the delightful anarchy of nature for a neat, human-enforced geometry. It uses up copious amounts of water and chemicals to feed specific, pliant species of grass at the expense of other living things. A lawn is scarified, aerated, tamed, shaved, manicured and soused with weedkiller that murders everything but grass. Not even the prettiest weeds, like daisies and speedwell, are spared.

An exam system is also a monoculture, because it only allows certain kinds of talent to grow. It looks nice and neat like a lawn, but it has killed beautiful things you will never see, such as those creative gifts that do not form into tidy shoots of learning. It has succumbed to our dictatorship of the countable, the way that we routinely give precedence to what can be measured. Not everything worth learning slots into skills gaps we have already decided we need to fill. Some things are too ineffable to turn into data, but that doesn't mean they don't matter or don't exist.

In graduation ceremonies at American colleges, a well-known speaker makes a commencement address. This address follows a set form, in which the speaker appears as an expert witness on the subject of failure. J. K. Rowling told Harvard graduates that after her own graduation she became 'the biggest failure I knew': a single mother with a brief marriage behind her, living on benefits. But this failure demanded 'a stripping away of the inessential'. She began to direct her energies into doing the only thing that mattered – writing about Harry Potter.

The talk show host Conan O'Brien spoke to Dartmouth College graduates about his failure to become host of *The Tonight Show*. It taught him, he said, that 'if you accept your misfortune and handle it right, your perceived failure can become a catalyst for profound reinvention'. Denzel Washington told University of Pennsylvania graduates about starring in a play in the same Broadway theatre where he'd failed his first audition thirty years earlier. 'Fall forward,' he counselled. 'Every failed experiment is one step closer to success.' Aaron Sorkin told Syracuse University graduates: 'Take risks, dare to fail, remember the first person through the wall always gets hurt.' Oprah Winfrey told Harvard graduates that 'there is no such thing as failure – failure is just life trying to move us in another direction'.

I am never likely to be asked to deliver a graduation address. But if the invite ever comes, I hope I would have the nerve to kill the mood a little.

'Esteemed chancellor, vice-chancellor, distinguished guests, graduands, ladies and gentlemen,' I would begin. 'I have sat through lots of these ceremonies and I know the drill. I, the honorary fellow, sit on a throne-like chair in my felt hat and velvety gown while the orator tells you how great I am. Then we doff our hats and he ushers me to the lectern so that you can all benefit from my wisdom. I address my remarks to the soon-to-be-graduates at the front. I tell them about my failures, and then order them not to be disheartened by theirs. *Don't be afraid to fail*, I say. *Failure is a gift. The only failure is being afraid to fail. I've spent a lifetime failing, but it's all been part of my journey to get here today.*

'At which point it may occur to you that this is an odd occasion to be talking about failure. Isn't the whole point of a graduation ceremony to shout about nailed-down, credentialled success? All through school, a battery of test scores has authenticated your achievements and your right to proceed to the next stage of your education. And now your degree certificate, that embossed piece of stiff paper with a crest and gold seal, hidden inside a cardboard cylinder like a pimped-up Pringles can, confirms your success to the world. Not that your polyester gowns and mortarboards can compete with the PhDs in their scarlet and gold robes, floppy felt hats and fur-lined hoods. Or the chancellor in his gold brocade and lace, his gown so heavy that he needs a trainbearer. A graduation ceremony is a festival of bling, and like all bling it bespeaks success.

'So when a speaker chooses this moment to hit you with a story of failure, be aware of the story's unspoken moral: this success is not enough. You will need to try and succeed again, and you will fail and fail again. In a meritocracy, even those who win need to carry on playing the game. The judgements keep coming all your life.

'I believe in meritocracy – up to a point. How could I be against exams, when I set and mark them? But I also believe in democracy. Democracy isn't about hoping to be one of the chosen; it's about being allowed to choose – to find your own way of living a meaningful life. The Greeks called it *eudaimonia*, or "human flourishing". To flourish means to flower, and flowers don't compete with each other. They flower in their own sweet way, without being told how to do it or measuring themselves against anything else. We are usually the best judges of how to use our own gifts.

'Each person has a deep reservoir of promise that we can't begin to fathom until it is fulfilled. When we are left to discover our own unknowable qualities, we tend to astound others and ourselves. Trust in your talents, and they will be a storehouse of solace all your life. It won't matter whether you fail or succeed at them by some conventional calculus or someone else's lights. Those who flourish rely on a different scale of values than the ordinary arithmetic of failure and success. So I won't lecture you today about how failure helped me get where I am, wherever that is. I will just say: congratulations on your success. May you use it to find your own way to flourish.'

4.

Life Is Hell, But at Least There Are Prizes

Or why rewards are never worth it

Once, in primary school, I was awarded three gold stars for a poem I wrote about a giant jam sandwich. These gold stars, laid out in rows on easy-peel sheets for the teacher to unpeel and stick to your work, were paltry things. But it was rare, perhaps unprecedented, to get three of them. So my teacher took me round all the other classrooms on a victory lap, while the other children had to stand and applaud.

I can remember, as she led me breezily through the school, both liking the attention and feeling hot with awkwardness. This had nothing to do with the fact that I had mostly plagiarized my poem from Janet Burroway's book *The Giant Jam Sandwich*, about which I felt no shame at all. It had more to do with me winning a race I had never agreed to enter. I felt the same about all the other school prizes I both wanted and didn't want, from spelling certificates to badges for learning my times tables. I longed to be singled out and sprinkled with praise, but not on other people's terms. The poet Mark Doty has written of 'the terrible dilemma of prizes: we cannot believe we deserve them, and we cannot quite believe we don't'.[1]

If I were an anthropologist of the modern workplace, I would start my fieldwork at an intriguing new phenomenon: the employee awards ceremony. These ceremonies model themselves on events like the BAFTAs and the Emmys, minus the chauffeured limousines, the red carpet and the flashing bulbs of the press photographers. They take place in hotel ballrooms with big screens, strobe lighting and corporate logos clearly displayed. A stand-up comic or other celebrity hosts for the evening, handing over awards made of moulded acrylic to 'inspirational leaders' and 'rising stars'.

Managers have an all-purpose phrase to explain this new feature of the workplace: *celebrating success*. I noted its sudden ubiquity in universities a few years ago when they started giving out vice-chancellor's medals to staff, for research and teaching 'excellence'. The words *celebrating success* suggest that no one has really competed for these prizes; success has just been benignly acknowledged from on high. Who but a killjoy would be against *celebrating success*?

Well then, I am a killjoy. I have always thought these awards patronizing and pernicious. The phrase *celebrating success* originated in primary schools, home of the easy-peel gold star. Now it has arrived in the world of work to infantilize us all. *Celebrating success* sets us in competition with our colleagues and gently badgers us into higher levels of performance. It sees our jobs not as a contract with our employers but as a life-ruling passion in which the best of us go 'above and beyond'.

The Dodo in *Alice's Adventures in Wonderland*, when asked who has won the Caucus race, declares: 'Everybody has won, and all must have prizes.' This being Wonderland, the Dodo is clearly talking nonsense. Everyone can't win a race, and if everyone gets a prize then the prize is meaningless. A prize is what economists call a positional good. Its value derives from its scarcity, the extent to which other people can't have it. Every time you give someone a prize, you're not giving it to everyone else. Every time you *celebrate success* you define what success is – and what failure is.

The workplace awards ceremony is a lazy substitute for genuine solicitude. It is cheaper and less trouble to give a few of your workers a prize than to waste time and money leading, motivating and caring about all of them. Better, too, for people to be competing for prizes than complaining about their insecure contracts or the gender pay gap. If I ever become a dictator, I will be sure to dish out lots of medals and honorifics to my subjects, to keep them busily competing for these awards and distracted from plotting my overthrow.

'Life is hell, but at least there are prizes.' So begins Janet Frame's story 'Prizes'. An unnamed narrator, not unlike Frame herself, greedily delineates the prizes she won at school, for handwriting, poetry and composition. Books bound in calf with the school motto on the flyleaf, scrolled certificates, postal orders for ten shillings: these are her means of escape from the 'status-free huddle' of her classmates. But at the story's end, now grown up and without the affirming edifices of school, she finds that she can 'no longer use prizes as a fortress'.[2] Who has she been competing with? Herself and everyone in the whole world, and neither of those races can be won. The prizes turn to bran and she is left alone and bereft, her life over.

As a shy person, though not as excruciatingly so as Frame was, I can see why she was drawn to prizes, since a knock-on effect of shyness is a failure to be memorable. The shy find it harder to make an impression on the world and are more likely to feel unheeded and unnoticed. I am a forgettable person. This is not self-deprecation but empirical observation, the evidence accumulated in live experiments over many years. Something about my face, voice and gait, the way I take up space in the world, fails to stick. I often need to reintroduce myself to someone I have already met, sometimes very recently. If they feel bad about having forgotten me, I pretend they are right and we haven't met after all. Once, at a conference, I had to re-explain who I was to someone who had been to the keynote lecture I had given earlier that day. He kept insisting that the lecture had been given by someone else, and after a while it seemed less trouble to agree with him.

So I, too, invisibilized and defeated by the amorphous judgements of social life, have craved the solidified esteem of a prize. A prize feels like something us shy people can bank and that may get us noticed – because we too are social animals, seeking appreciation as much as anyone. A prize looks like a voucher we can swap in the real world for acceptance and approval. Or at least it does some of the time, when we are not being the social sceptics and non-joiners that shy people also often are. We know deep down, even as we try to purchase self-worth in the currency of teachers' ticks and sticky gold stars, that it will never be enough. The endless quest for prizes will only make us feel more like failures.

In 1938, Virginia Woolf, filled with fear about a looming world war, published a long, angry essay called *Three Guineas*. The book is an imagined response to three letters that Woolf receives asking for advice: one from an 'educated gentleman' on how to prevent war, one from a women's league on how to help women enter the professions, and one from a women's college building fund on how to encourage women into higher education. All three letter-writers are angling for a financial donation – the three guineas of the title. Instead Woolf donates her thoughts, as a woman largely excluded from formal education, about male power.

Three Guineas is illustrated with photographs of important-looking men in full fig. An old general on parade wears a jacket weighed down with medals and ribbons. An archbishop leads a procession, dressed in his episcopal vestments and holding a sceptre and cross. A judge walks down the courtroom steps in wig and robe. University dons walk in line, dressed in robes and tasselled hats and carrying maces. Woolf saw all this as peacocking: the chronic male need to proclaim one's pre-eminence. She found it – in a leap that some of her readers found a bit much – fascistic, part of the same macho culture that was leading the world to war.

The wearing of ribbons, bits of metal and tufts of fur, Woolf writes, is 'a barbarity which deserves the ridicule which we bestow upon the rites of savages'. She urges women not to join in this male obsession with honours. Women, she points out, have been well trained by a patriarchy suspicious of all female self-advertisement. They should form a 'society of outsiders', indifferent to these 'baubles and labels by which brain merit is advertised and certified'.[3]

'Brain merit' is an inspired phrase. How absurd it is, those words imply, to reward people for having a well-functioning body organ, as absurd as awarding medals for outstanding livers or exceptional spleens. Woolf looks hard at the glittering prizes of the intellectual elite, of which she was certainly a part, and breaks their spell. Seen with her outsider's eye, all their symbolism burns away like morning mist and they seem suddenly pointless and sad.

Since the Bronze Age, people have honoured their heroes and rulers by covering them in gold. Gold was used to adorn the human body long before it was used as money. The way that its deep, sunlight yellow emerged out of colourless earth and rock, and the blacksmith's fire, must have seemed a kind of magic.

In August 1876, the archaeologist and adventurer Heinrich Schliemann began digging, on a hunch, near the walls of the ancient city of Mycenae in southern Greece. There he discovered deep shafts, at the bottom of which were the graves of ancient warriors. A few years earlier, he had excavated at Hisarlik in northwest Turkey and found the Homeric city of Troy. He had moved on to Mycenae inspired by Homer's account of it as 'abounding in gold'. In these shaft graves, nearly 4,000 years old, he found human skeletons and mummified bodies, wrapped in burial shrouds of gold foil and covered with thin-beaten gold objects. There were gold rings with inset gems on their fingers and gold bracelets around their wrists. On their ribcages were gold medallions, with intricate repoussé designs of flowers, butterflies and cuttlefish. Gold diadems and death masks covered their skulls. Schliemann believed one of these bodies to be Agamemnon, the gold-encrusted king of Mycenae in the *Iliad*. The ancients glorified and decorated their heroes even in death.

The gold medal originates in war. The Roman Empire awarded its soldiers medals called *phalerae*: bronze, silver or gold discs worn on their armour. Civilian medals first spread among the rulers of northern Italy in the early fifteenth century. Emulating the example of coins with Caesar's head on them, these medals honoured the ruler or great man shown on the front, in a revival of antiquity's ideals of splendid human achievement. Louis XIV of France commissioned hundreds of medals, depicting him winning heroic victories in battle, shining as the Sun King on the earth below or steering his chariot through the skies.

In the early days, medal-makers cast a mould and poured hot metal into it. Each mould was used only once, so medals were only made in small numbers. With the arrival of die-stamping machines in the 1550s, though, the design could easily be imprinted on the medal and even more medals were struck. In the nineteenth century, machine cutters speeded things up further. Now there were many more medals, for valorous soldiers, victorious athletes and illustrious scholars – an industrial revolution in celebrating success.

Gold is mostly useless, being too heavy for weaponry and too soft for tools. We prize it for two reasons. First, its rarity: all the gold ever mined would fit into a largish university lecture theatre. Second, its durability: gold may be soft but it is nigh on indestructible. An unreactive element, it does not tarnish, like silver or bronze, on contact with the gases in the air. In its rarity and durability, gold has come to stand for rare and durable achievement – as an emblem of eternity.

In Wagner's *Ring Cycle*, the magic ring, forged by the dwarf

Alberich from Rhinegold stolen from the Rhine maidens, has no great intrinsic value. What makes it covetable, and gives its owner the power to rule the world, is that everyone is fighting over it. Just as success must be collectively agreed before it becomes success, gold is prized for being prized.

When *Three Guineas* was published, many critics were puzzled. They expressed surprise, as critics have ever since, that Virginia Woolf, a writer already assured of lasting renown, could see herself as an outsider – part of what she called 'the ignorantsia'.[4] But it is not surprising at all. In Woolf's diaries, the word *failure* appears again and again like an incantation. All her life she thought herself a failed writer and a failed woman. 'I could not write, and all the devils came out – hairy black ones,' she wrote to her sister Vanessa on 8 June 1911. 'To be 29 and unmarried – to be a failure – childless – insane too, no writer.' Getting married did not still these thoughts: she saw her childlessness as yet another failure.

Nor did being published help. She routinely lost faith in a book after finishing it, her breakdowns often overlapping with publication. One of her first diary entries, on 27 January 1915, mentions her first novel, *The Voyage Out*, 'which everyone, so I predict will assure me is the most brilliant thing they've ever read; & privately condemn, as indeed it deserves to be condemned'. On 31 December 1940, while finishing her last novel, *Between the Acts*, she wrote to her doctor, Octavia Wilberforce, that it was 'an unborn and as far as I can tell completely worthless book'.

But Woolf also knew that the art she wanted to make could not happen without the risk of failure. Beauty, she wrote on Christmas Day 1922 to a dejected younger writer, Gerald Brenan, 'is only got by the failure to get it; by grinding all the flints together; by facing what must be humiliation – the things one can't do – To aim at beauty deliberately, without this apparently insensate struggle, would result, I think, in little daisies and forget-me-nots – simpering sweetnesses.'

Woolf's modernism was bound to 'fail' on one level, because it risked the perplexity of her readers. It meant doing away with audience-pleasing platitudes, breaking through the wall of social convention to explore how we really think and feel when words fail us. Anyone willing to embark on a biography of Elizabeth Barrett Browning's cocker spaniel (*Flush*), a historical epic in which the title character changes sex and lives for over 300 years (*Orlando*) or a novel-collage of broken impressions of an ordinary June day in London (*Mrs Dalloway*) must have known that she might fail.

Mrs Dalloway is itself a book about failure. At fifty-three, Peter Walsh surveys the wreckage of his life: sent down from Oxford, literary ambitions come to nothing, rejected by Clarissa Dalloway, married on the rebound, now a jobless widower hoping to cadge a sinecure. Sally Seton has given up her vibrant, bisexual youth for a sexless marriage. Hugh Whitbread, a minor court official, attracts sniggers from his friends for dressing in lace ruffles and knee breeches. Clarissa's husband, Richard, a Member of Parliament once tipped for high office, is not even a junior minister.

But these characters are redeemed by their failures, which make them more human. The novel's successful professional men, by contrast, are all smugly convinced that they will never be floored by life. Two pompous medics, Dr Holmes and Sir William Bradshaw, treat a suicidal man with cheery perfunctoriness. A puffed-up Milton scholar, Professor Brierly, is incapable of sustaining small talk at Clarissa's party with a man who has not been classically trained. One imagines these Supreme Beings speaking in the braying tone that Woolf so hated in the men she met.

As for Clarissa, everyone sees her as a chic hostess, 'but failure one conceals'. She knows that she is poorly educated, can't write or play the piano and doesn't know where or even what the equator is. She can do one thing well: turn the parties she hosts into something graceful and joyous, briefly illumining her existence and that of her friends. But is this enough to show for her time on earth? She feels 'the dwindling of life; how year by year her share was sliced'.

In one brief passage, Clarissa remembers being a little girl, throwing bread to the ducks near a lake while her mother and father look on. Then suddenly she sees herself as a grown woman in the same place, walking towards her parents, cradling her life in her arms as it grew bigger and bigger 'until it became a whole life, a complete life, which she put down by them and said, "This is what I have made of it! This!" And what had she made of it? What, indeed?'

What, indeed? We cling to prizes as proof: the certification that we have spent our time on earth wisely and well. They are the till receipt us failures forgot to ask for at the cash register of life, or were never offered. *This is what I have made of my life . . . this!* But even those who receive such certification may find it wanting. Success is too shapeless a thing to be frozen into a prize – just as we could never bundle up something as curious and uncontainable as a life and hold it in our hands.

According to the French philosopher René Girard, human beings are driven by 'mimetic desire'. Once we have met our creaturely needs – food, water, shelter, sleep – the power of mimicry takes over. Not only do we want what others want or already have, we want it *because* they want it or already have it. By acquiring it, we hope that we will also acquire those enviable assets – wisdom, happiness, nonchalance, existential certitude – that we are so sure others possess and we do not. Mimetic desire strengthens human bonds but also foments rivalries, as we all end up wanting the same things.

When we mimic each other's desires like this, desire can never be slaked. Mimetic desire, for Girard, has three parts: a desirer, an object of desire (such as a gold medal) and a mediator who serves as the rival for that object. 'The object is to the mediator what the relic is to a saint,' he writes.[5] 'External' mediation occurs when we try to mimic some distant hero or heroine, and is fairly harmless. 'Internal' mediation is more dangerous: the desirer and the mediator know each other and their rivalry may eclipse the object of desire. Since mimetic desire is unconscious and pre-rational, we desirers do not notice the mediator who comes between us and that coveted object. Girard calls this blindness 'the romantic lie'. We think we want the object, but actually we want the charismatic quality we assign to the rival who also wants or already possesses that object. Mimetic desire is asking for the impossible: for us to be someone else.

Girard supports his theory with readings of classic literature. Don Quixote's ambition to be a knight springs, he argues, from his need to imitate a fictional chivalric hero, Amadis of Gaul. Julien Sorel's love affairs and misadventures in Stendhal's novel *The Red and the Black* all flow from his mimetic desire for Napoleon, whose memoirs he hides under his mattress. Madame Bovary worships not her lovers but the protagonists of romantic novels she read as a girl. In Proust, men desire women, as Swann loves Odette, 'because of the counterpoise of all the men with whom we have to compete for them'.[6]

These characters all learn what we will learn. When we reach our goal and the rival falls away, the prize loses its lustre. That hunted-after truffle, hidden under the ground and so delectable in prospect, tastes only of mud and truffle hog's breath. Prizes make no one happy, even those who win them. 'Everyone knows that all medals are rubber,' wrote the poet Donald Hall, after queueing up at the White House to receive a National Medal of the Arts from Barack Obama.[7] The need for accolades is irrational and can't be reasoned away. Our head tells us that a prize will solve nothing, and will still leave us with our life, and all its blotches and blemishes, where it was. Our heart wants it anyway.

One of Girard's students at Stanford in the late 1980s was Peter Thiel, later a billionaire venture capitalist and co-founder of PayPal. Thiel credited Girard's work as an inspiration. It taught him, he said, how herd-like people are, and how much entrepreneurs could gain from not following the herd. It also convinced him of the market potential of social networks based on mimetic desire. He was the first big investor in Facebook, buying 10 per cent of the company for $500,000, one of the most lucrative angel investments ever. Viral marketing on social media relies on the Girardian principle of desire stirred by some captivating stranger, an *influencer*. Girard has been called 'the godfather of the Like button'.

In the early days of social media we had 'friends'; now we have 'followers'. Online, we get sucked into celebrating our own success and inciting the mimetic rivalry of our followers. The virtual world has scrambled our sense of tact and decorum in these matters. No one starts a real-world conversation with 'Listen to this great thing that someone said about me!' But online, people share praise, or praise themselves, all the time. *Super-excited to announce*, they write, or *Thrilled to share this news*. Some do it shyly, with a *So this happened* or a *Shameless self-promotion klaxon*. They still do it. The humblebrag has regressed to its more primitive form, the brag. Nowadays no one can be bothered to dress a boast in the garb of fake humility. The short messages we post online are called, fittingly, status updates. Under the alibi of sharing information, they seek to enhance the author's standing among the electronic tribe. They hide our imperfect lives behind a curated collage of them.

If you are feeling like a failure, the cumulative effect can be draining. Your timeline fills up with a ceaseless procession of people accepting awards, holding up certificates, quoting lines from reviews of their books and sharing news of their job promotions. How little they know of human psychology if they believe that the distant colleagues and virtual strangers who follow them online are longing to read an inventory of their achievements.

But that self-praising status updater is not so different from us – and, on another day, may even be us. We all dread, most of all, not being loved. To a human being, that can feel like annihilation. All our lives we are searching for a spell to keep at bay the indifference of others, our deep dread at being overlooked. Prizes work on this deficit model. We worry that without them we will feel ignored and discounted, left outside the circle of grace. 'People are afraid that all people are equal,' John Freccero, Dante scholar and lifelong friend of René Girard, says.[8] We seek the invidious distinction of prizes because we fear that we are no better than anyone else. Our fear is well founded. The hardest news to take is that we are just human, with nothing exceptional about either our talents or our foibles, and that this should be – can only be – enough.

Just missing out on a medal is worst of all. Coming fourth has none of the weird distinction, the inverted glamour even, of coming last. In her photo series *Fourth*, the Australian artist Tracey Moffatt pictures Olympians finishing fourth at the 2000 Sydney Olympics. This project was itself a kind of failure for Moffatt. She had been sounded out three years earlier to be the official Olympic photographer but they never rang back. She ended up watching it all on television. She also asked friends in different countries to record the entire games and send her the tapes. She knew that cameras tend to focus on the winners and spreading the net like this would give her more chance of catching the losers. She spent days watching the recorded footage, with her finger on the pause button. When she spotted a fourth-placed athlete, she froze the screen and took a picture.

Fourth includes twenty-six of these photos, grainy shots printed on small canvas squares and coated with varnish so they look like paintings. Each image captures that grave moment when a competitor has just finished their event and it dawns on them that they have come fourth. Against a greenish monochrome background they appear in colour, as if a bright force field of failure surrounds them. A defeated long-distance runner holds his hands up to cover his face. An exhausted swimmer hovers at the back of the shot as a grinning medal winner points at her friends in the stands. A Ukrainian also-ran looks up at the results board where his fate is sealed in dot-matrix numbers. A judo player lies flat on the mat, floored by the opponent who now rejoices at his bronze medal. A runner has no strength left to shake the hand of the victor, touching it briefly instead. Another athlete is patted by a disembodied arm.

Since Moffatt doesn't identify these fourth-placed Olympians by name, she clearly isn't interested in giving them the moment of immortality they missed out on. Instead they come to stand for something universal and ecumenical about the human response to failure. The faces of those who came fourth are blank, with a look aimed very far away. Moffatt described this face as 'an awful, beautiful, knowing mask, which says "Oh shit!"'[9] There is too much going on in that moment for tears to fall, the emotional pain having yet to catch up with the physical pain. The lungs are gasping for oxygen, the muscles are full of lactic acid and the body is screaming at the brain: 'What have you done to me? Why didn't you stop when I told you to?' And the pain is so much worse when it has all been for nothing.

In elite sport, the margins between success and failure are vanishingly small. Electronic starting pistols and laser finishing lines can accurately separate athletes by millionths of a second. The minutest fractions police the border between elation and desolation, killing all perspective. If you came fourth, you can't be consoled with the thought that you were one of the small band of exceptionally athletic humans who made it to an Olympic final or that just to be an Olympian is to be grouped with the gods of ancient Greece. So what? You came fourth. You have been herded into the homogeny of the unplaced.

What happens after you come fourth says it all. The camera, which only caught you by accident, quickly moves on to the winner, now draped in the national flag and doing a victory lap, pursued by presenters with microphones who brush past you as if you don't exist. When you fly home, you have to stay on the plane while they photograph the winners on the boarding stairs, biting down on their medals. Your sponsorship deals get quietly dropped; your lottery funding instantly dries up. Requests to appear in adverts for energy drinks are redirected. On the motivational speech circuit, only the gold medallists get to give advice about dealing with failure – because failure must always be reshaped into that timeless sporting trope, the redemptive arc. You, the true authority on failure, have been disappeared.

I remember one of those fourth places well, although it doesn't appear in Moffatt's series. I stayed up into the early hours on a Friday night – Saturday morning in Sydney – to see if the veteran British rower Steve Redgrave could win his fifth Olympic gold medal. I recall almost nothing about that race, except that he did. But an hour earlier, at midnight, I watched another race that has stuck in my head ever since.

Ed Coode and Greg Searle were rowing for Britain in the coxless pairs and were tipped for gold. They started well and after the first quarter led the field by more than two seconds. But then, about halfway, they began to tire. The French crew passed them, unstoppably, and they found themselves in a desperate fight for silver or bronze.

Rowers know in their guts and bones when a race is lost. In training, they perfect a technique of releasing the blade from the water and rotating it ready for the next stroke, to reduce splash and make the boat glide with minimal friction through the water. But in a race, tiredness and tension take over and this technique deteriorates just as it needs to improve. Instead of being a continuous, fluid motion, the rowing stroke gets choppy and the boat slows up.

Watching on television was agonizing, because the bow of a rowing boat bobs back a little after each stroke nudges it forward. Different camera angles seemed to show Coode and Searle slightly behind or slightly ahead. They were second until the last stroke, when both the Americans and Australians edged past them by inches.

The three medal-winning crews paddled to the shore, keen to meet up with their supporters. Coode and Searle just floated alone in the middle of the lake. Searle put his head in his hands and wept, then lay back, his head cradled in Coode's arms. They looked around, bemused – as if they were waiting for someone to tell them that it was all a mistake and that they had won after all. But after a few minutes Searle reached back and touched Coode's leg, and they rowed off the lake with oars made of lead.

During the ensuing television interview, they struggled to make sense of what had happened. Had they started too fast? They did not think so; they were going full pelt at the end. They hadn't bottled it or blown it. They just hadn't won. All they had wanted was gold, and now they were distraught at having no medal at all. Coode, who had seemed the more collected of the two, broke down in tears. 'I just can't believe we've come away with nothing after three years,' he said. After an excruciating pause, the flustered interviewer said something about this being what an Olympic final was all about. To watch such raw hurt, unglazed by good manners, felt like intruding on grief.

Coode and Searle were surely grieving not just for that stab of pain at the finishing line but for all those dark mornings on the freezing Thames, all those lonely afternoons on rowing machines. Six hours every day holding an oar handle or a weights bar – and all for an ever-aching back, stomach ulcers, ligament tears, hands pocked with blisters and legs full of cuts from the seat tracks. Olympic rowers wreck their bodies in search of some brittle dream of glory over just six minutes on the water. Elite sport is mostly boredom mixed with agony, endured in the hope of a single victory that may come years later, if at all. Only in sport is such monomania deemed laudable instead of crazy.

Since that midnight race at the Sydney Olympics, I have made a point of looking out for the losers. Tennis players with towels over their heads, rueing that last, unforced error, a fluffed volley into the net on match point. Cricketers replaying the straight-bat shot that edged to first slip, as they slope back to the pavilion on a duck, shaking their heads. Footballers down on their haunches, or burying their heads in the turf, while their opponents victory-dance and high-five around them. Bloodied rugby players stood with hands on hips and heads bowed, their eyes wet but refusing to weep. Defeat always feels more revealing, more pitilessly exposing, than victory.

I had forgotten – until I just looked it up – that four years later, in Athens, Coode won a gold medal. I had also forgotten that Searle had already won gold, at the previous Olympics, and went on to win another bronze. I only remembered their coming fourth and their haunted looks that day. Much later, I came across a description of the defeated Olympians of ancient Greece in one of Pindar's odes, which reminded me of them. 'Nor when they returned to their mothers did sweet laughter bring them joy,' it went, 'but steering clear of their foes they cowered in back alleys, pierced by failure.'

One mild, mid September morning towards the end of her life, Virginia Woolf was reading in her study at Monk's House, her country retreat in Rodmell, Sussex. Through the window she could see life going on: a farmer ploughing a nearby field, rooks rising out of the trees. Then out of the corner of her eye she spotted a day moth fluttering on a square of the windowpane. Woolf had long been fascinated by lepidoptera. As children, she and her brother and sister would trap and sedate them.

But she had work to do, and so she carried on reading. Then, looking up again, she noticed that the moth's movements had become stiff. After a few more failed stabs at flight, it fell flat on its back on the windowsill, its little legs pedalling uselessly. Woolf stretched out a pencil to right it, but then saw that the moth was dying, and laid the pencil down. This moth was not about to be rewarded for its persistence like the spider in the Scottish cave that spun a web after many failed attempts, inspiring Robert the Bruce to fight on against the English. Woolf's moth was just dying banally one autumn morning. A day moth's life is short.

Just before its last breath, though, the moth had one marvellous final rally in which it managed to right itself. 'When there was nobody to care or to know,' Woolf wrote, 'this gigantic effort on the part of an insignificant little moth, against a power of such magnitude, to retain what no one else valued or desired to keep, moved one strangely.'

No one seems to know for sure when Woolf watched that dying moth, or even when she wrote the essay 'The Death of the Moth', which so lovingly chronicles its last hours. It was found in her papers and published in 1942, a year after her death. Most likely, the moth breathed its last in September 1940, when the Woolfs were staying at Monk's House. The war that she dreaded in *Three Guineas* had arrived and was now terrifyingly close. The Battle of Britain had been waging above Rodmell since the middle of July. On 11 September, just before tea, she and her husband, Leonard, saw a German plane shot down over Lewes racecourse, followed by a cloud of thick black smoke. By then the Blitz had begun as well, and they heard German bombers flying over at night on their way to London. In mid September, their house in Mecklenburgh Square, Bloomsbury, was badly hit. A dying moth was an odd thing for Woolf to be fixating on, that autumn morning.

But Woolf was not only writing about that moth. She would have known that the classical Greek word for the human soul and for a moth is the same: *psyche*. Literally, the word means *breath*. The moth in Woolf's essay stands for the breath of life, stripped of human investments and appurtenances, life without prizes or brickbats, victories or defeats – life as just a little blob of awareness and appetite.

'One is apt to forget all about life, seeing it humped and bossed and garnished and cumbered so that it has to move with the greatest circumspection and dignity,' she writes. If those men pictured in the photographic plates for *Three Guineas* stand for life garnished and cumbered, then this moth stands for life in its plainest form. Woolf is careful to say how ordinary her moth looks, neither 'gay' like a butterfly nor 'sombre' like a night moth, its only decoration the tassel fringes on its hay-coloured wings. 'It was as if someone had taken a tiny bead of pure life,' she goes on, 'and decking it as lightly as possible with down and feathers, had set it dancing and zig-zagging to show us the true nature of life.'

'The Death of the Moth' is a song in praise of sheer existence, of a life that counts for nothing but itself. As for those defeated Olympic rowers, all they had spent those years in achieving – the podium finish, the medals and bouquets, the flag raised for the national anthem – was a puny human construct. This only made their failure more devastating. They couldn't be comforted because they were fighting their own battles, for tenuous meanings and symbols into which they had poured their hearts. The pursuit of laurel leaves is always lonely-making. Woolf reminds us that life in its unadulterated essence – as animating breath and animal sensation – is already precious and beyond price. Nothing else matters in the end.

*

According to the Dutch historian Johan Huizinga, a defining quality of humans is our playfulness. In his 1938 book *Homo Ludens*, Huizinga argues that the ethos of play is egalitarian. Play must be voluntary and the rules the same for everyone, and no material gain can be had from it. It never involves competing for things that matter, such as money, land or power. It is done with absolute seriousness but with an underlying awareness of its ultimate futility. It is a beautifully useless adornment to life, a simple celebration of human vitality, elegance and grace.

Play is finite, its limits fixed. It takes place within an agreed playground, enclosed by actual white lines or ones painted in the mind, where everyone agrees to follow the same rules. These rules allow play to cast its spell over us for a short while. They enchant us into thinking that what goes on in the playground really matters. Then the referee's whistle breaks the spell and real life resumes.

It used to puzzle me why footballers celebrate goals, which are only a partial victory, more hungrily than they do the final whistle, when victory is assured. Now I see why: a goal is more than just a numerical adjustment to the scoreline. Within the rules of the game, it doesn't matter how a goal is scored, only that the entire ball crosses the goal line. But still we respond more ecstatically to the ball that, tracing a perfect parabola, dips over the defensive wall to make a satisfying ripple in the top corner of the net than to the ball that dribbles across the line after glancing off a defender's bum cheek. Sport's best moments are never just about victory. They are about play, the way that a luminous piece of skill emerges out of the half-choreographed dance of collective movement. The final whistle, however thrilling the victory it confirms, declares that play is over. Nothing afterwards, even the lifting of a trophy, can match the life-giving joy of play.

Play reminds us that it is okay to care about something too deeply, and then for this useless overinvestment to come to a healthy and nourishing end. In play, no one dies, winning isn't everything and losing is no disgrace. The custom of both winner and loser shaking hands at the close of a game is a hat-tip to time and tide – and to the reality that no feeling, either euphoria or despair, lasts.

Play's basic covenant is that it ends. Play is not play unless its spell can be broken and we can return to normality. Any prize we might win from play is worthless in the long run. You can't convert the currency of play into the currency of the outside world, any more than you can pay a restaurant bill with Monopoly money. We should care about winning only until the game is over, or just a little while after that, and then get on with the rest of our lives. When the prize is all that matters, sport becomes a bleak duty and defeat a needless humiliation – masochism in search of a medal.

The sporting masochists want only to win. They buy into a whole belief system about motivation, positive mental attitude and that fugue state of being 'in the zone'. The mere thought of losing must be banished for good. The most shaming identity for a sporting masochist, worse than being a cheat, is being a choker: someone who lost because they let negativity control them.

These sporting masochists also put their faith in technology. Many a goal celebration is now cut short by the referee jogging to pitchside to examine the build-up via VAR (video assistant referee), only to find that the goal scorer was offside by the length of a kneecap. VAR came in after the top clubs petitioned for it. They needed to see a commercial return on the fortunes they had invested in their squads and were naturally enraged when erratic refereeing (as they saw it) cost them games. And so a rule devised to stop forwards from goal-hanging now comes down to the precise measurement of protruding body parts.

The sporting masochists are seeking technocratic perfection

in an imperfect world. They wish to turn the rules of the game, which are no more than codes and conventions, into legal and scientific laws. VAR loathes ambiguity, even when the destruction of ambiguity also destroys the cathartic release of play. Fans in the stadium now celebrate goals more mutedly, in case those celebrations prove premature. While the game stops and everyone waits for VAR to deliver its verdict, they have taken to protest-chanting: 'It's not football any more.'

Predictably, VAR has not rid the game of arguments, nor of the excuses that the sporting masochists come up with for losing games – such as that the ball was too bouncy, or too light, or the floodlights were too bright, or the pitch was too dry, or the referee broke up the rhythm of the game with his constant whistling, or the ball boys didn't return the ball quickly enough, or the players couldn't see each other in their new strip, to name just a few of the mitigations I have heard from football managers over the years. Nor has VAR done away with that undying post-match tradition, the losing manager's rant at the referee.

For in sport, as in life, we are all at the mercy of contingency. A victor needs to be lucky – especially in the non-stop, fluid, error-ridden sport of football, where goals are rare and a dodgy deflection or goalkeeper's fumble can decide a game. It doesn't matter how hard you train, how positive your mantras are, how smart the technology is. Sometimes – most of the time – you will fail. Thirty-one of the thirty-two football teams in the World Cup finals fail. 126 of the 128 men and women in the Wimbledon singles fail. 155 of the 156 golfers in the British Open fail – not counting all the qualifying rounds, where many more fail in the shadows.

Edward de Bono, the champion of lateral thinking, devised a mental shortcut for working out how many matches you need to organize if, say, you are running a knockout tennis tournament with 111 entrants. When faced with this sort of task, most people draw little diagrams with the pairings for each match, or work back from the final to the semi-finals, and so on. But all you need do is shift your attention from the winner of each match to the loser, in whom no one is usually interested. Each match has one loser and each loser can lose only once – so there must be 110 losers and therefore 110 matches.[10] In sport, almost everyone loses. Without the likelihood of defeat, and the uncertainty of victory, sport would be unwatchable.

Sport has become so much about winning that we have forgotten its true point: play. We know instinctively when we see children abandoned in play that they have found the secret to life that we have lost. The liberation theologian Dorothee Sölle was once asked how she would explain happiness to a child. 'I wouldn't explain it,' she replied. 'I'd toss him a ball and let him play.'[11] The same impulse exists in other animals, in the just-for-the-hell-of-it way that a crane leaps up like a ballet dancer executing an entrechat or a young raven drops a stick in mid-air and dives to catch it again. True happiness never comes from pursuing prizes – because any prize that might be won will soon retreat into a past life we can't retrieve. It comes from fully absorbing ourselves in this one irretrievable moment of being alive on this earth. The priceless things in life can't be held on to, only lived.

On 19 June 1974, the Netherlands were playing Sweden in a group match in the World Cup finals at the Westfalenstadion in Dortmund. Twenty-three minutes into the game, an aerial ball arrived at the Dutch player Johan Cruyff's feet. Cruyff was to the left of the Swedish penalty area, with his back to the goal line, the hefty right-back Jan Olsson marking him tightly. By dropping his left shoulder, Cruyff fooled Olsson into thinking that he was about to cross with his right foot. As Olsson moved to block the cross, Cruyff dragged the ball back behind his planted left foot with his right instep, while simultaneously turning his body 180 degrees. In a half-second he was clear and skipping to the goal line with the ball. Olsson, as baffled as everyone else as to what had just occurred, almost fell over.

Nowadays football matches can be cut up into little video-clip memes – a balletic save, an acrobatic volley, a fifty-yard run that leaves a line of breathless defenders in its wake – and shared online. But back then there was only the slow-motion action replay to go on. It took several showings of it for the commentators to work out how Cruyff had executed this move – one that, once seen, seemed such a perfect union of form and function that it was odd no one had tried it before. Later, in the Swedish dressing room, Olsson and his teammates could only laugh at its chutzpah. Meanwhile thousands of boys around the world were already outside, in streets and back gardens, practising the 'Cruyff turn'.

Rudolf Nureyev said that Cruyff, with his hip swivels and tip-toe shuffles, should have been a ballet dancer. Cruyff knew that the secret of a great footballer, as with a great dancer, is balance. He had perfected his own by playing as a boy in the Amsterdam streets without studs, spending many hours trying not to fall on the concrete flags. Nureyev and Cruyff even looked a little alike, with cheekbones that made their resting faces look imperious. Cruyff once said that the best footballers reveal their character in their style of play. With the Cruyff turn, he revealed his. He had not perfected it in training, as a way of wowing the crowd or humbling his opponent. He had simply found, in an unrehearsed slice of counter-intuition, the easiest way to beat his man.

Even so, there is no escaping it: the Cruyff turn failed. After he left the Swedish defender flailing, Cruyff curved a cross with the outside of his right foot towards the Dutch forward, Johnny Rep, who, as surprised as anyone, completely missed the ball. It ran on to another Dutch player, Wim van Hanegem, who ran straight into a defender and fell over. The ball was cleared.

The Cruyff turn became just one of the hundreds of moments in any football match that come to nothing. A striker toe-ends the ball tamely at the keeper, or blazes it over the bar, or loses it in a scramble of bodies and a defender hoicks it into touch. All the players traipse back up the pitch to start over again. Sport, like life, is mostly wasted breath. The Sweden–Netherlands game ended 0–0, the only match in the tournament in which the Netherlands failed to score. Both teams ended up qualifying from the group in any case, so the match didn't even matter. The Netherlands made it to the final, where they were beaten by West Germany. The Cruyff turn was a beautiful failure, rather like the Dutch team itself – probably the best side not to win the World Cup, and certainly better than many that did.

Even in Huizinga's time, the regimentation of sport was undermining the spontaneity of play. In his book *Football in Sun and Shadow*, Eduardo Galeano writes that 'the history of football is a sad voyage from beauty to duty'.[12] For Galeano, the professional game had turned winning into a joyless obligation. By the early 1970s, when the Dutch brand of total football arrived like a reviving breeze, the game was being strangled by the need to win at all costs. English football had perfected the art of the professional foul, the cynical trade of a yellow card for preventing a goal. Italian football had pioneered a play-safe mode, deploying a sweeper, man-to-man marking and lots of sideways passing in an attempt to win every match 1–0. Widely copied, these innovations were choking the fun out of the game.

Bill Shankly, manager of Liverpool FC, encapsulated the winner's ethos in his famous saying: 'First is first, second is nowhere.' Kevin Keegan, who played under Shankly, wrote later that the open-top bus parades when they brought trophies back to the city made him feel as if they were in ancient Rome, 'like warriors returning from a bloody conquest to show off all the gold and loot we had plundered'.[13] Trophies (from the Greek root *trope*, for 'rout') derive from the ancient practice of displaying in a public place the weapons, and sometimes the body parts, of beaten enemies. To the victor the spoils; to the vanquished the shame.

For Cruyff's Dutch team, though, winning the trophy seemed like a mere detail. Of the 1974 final, Johnny Rep said that 'we kind of forgot we had to win, which was a shame'. Not that they didn't want to win. There were tears in the Dutch dressing room after that final, just as in every losing finalists' dressing room before and since. But Cruyff and his team believed that if winning was everything then it was no longer worth having. If they couldn't win beautifully, they preferred to fail beautifully.

Later, as coach of Ajax and Barcelona, Cruyff challenged the then risk-averse and failure-fearing tactics of professional football. He urged his goalkeepers to act like an extra outfield player, an eleventh man, coming out of the penalty area to sweep up loose balls, pass the ball out and start attacks. Goalkeeping is a friendless and thankless trade: every mistake risks being punished with a goal. Cruyff noticed that, as a breed, keepers were chary of coming too far out of their goal because they feared being beaten by a ball lobbed over their head from long distance, which would make them look stupid. But that happened rarely, and the gamble was worth taking for the sake of nipping attacks in the bud and starting new moves. The keeper, and the team, had to risk spectacular failure for the sake of less visible gains.

Often, when watching from the touchline as coach, Cruyff forgot the score. What mattered was that, win or lose, his teams play football. By then he knew that although his Dutch team of 1974 had lost, they had won a bigger victory by playing football the world still talked about. 'There is no medal better than being acclaimed for your style,' he said. The Cruyff turn was a failure in all ways except one: every football fan remembers it, or has seen it, or heard about it. Imagine sport without moments like these. It would just be bare stats, a binary account of wins and losses, with all the romance of a spreadsheet.

*

In *The Boys of Summer*, his classic account of the great Brooklyn Dodgers baseball team of the early 1950s, Roger Kahn reflects on the unlooked-for splendour of sporting failure. Kahn recalls how, when he started reporting their matches for the *New York Herald*, the team 'twitched in shock and mortification'. No major-league baseball team had made so little of its stupendous talents. Twice they had lost the league pennant in the final inning of the final game of the season. This flair for last-ditch defeat carried on in the two seasons Kahn followed them, in both of which they lost the World Series to the New York Yankees. But the Dodgers did not fail because of some dearth of courage or determination, he decides. They were just unlucky, and 'choker and hero are two masks for the same plain face'.

The Dodgers did manage a lone World Series win in 1955. But the great team soon dispersed, through the usual sporting attrition of loss of form, injury, ageing and retirement – and, in 1957, the owner of the Dodgers relocating them to Los Angeles. Kahn's title, *The Boys of Summer*, comes from a line in a Dylan Thomas poem about the fleetingness of youthful glory. A ball player, Kahn writes, 'must confront two deaths'. The first reckoning comes in his thirties, when his major-league reflexes leave him and he dies as an athlete. Twenty years after their prime, Kahn talks to some of the players, including the great Jackie Robinson, the first black player in the major leagues. He sees his baseball gods grown into mortals, but handling their demotion with courage and dignity. This makes them, he argues, all the more worthy of his veneration.

Only the literal-minded think that sport is all about winning; its subtext always says something more acute and profound. 'You may glory in a team triumphant, but you fall in love with a team in defeat,' Kahn writes. 'Losing after great striving is the story of man, who was born to sorrow, whose sweetest songs tell of saddest thought, and who, if he is a hero, does nothing in life as becomingly as leaving it.'[14]

*

Those who don't know much about Virginia Woolf know two things about her. The first is that she was a snob – which is true in the limited sense that she was an upper-middle-class English-woman with the sometimes ugly prejudices of her class and time. Unlike most snobs, though, she was self-diagnosed. In her 1936 essay 'Am I a Snob?', she confessed that if she received a letter stamped with a coronet it would always float to the top of her letter pile, even though she knew that none of her friends cared about such things. This proved, she wrote, that 'like a rash or a spot . . . I have the disease'.[15]

But Woolf also had in spades that fail-safe counteragent to snobbery, curiosity. When we are curious about what it is like to be another human being, or even a moth, our mood turns generous and gently probing. We lose any interest in comparing that life to ours or judging it a success or failure. We notice it instead for the irreducible and inestimable thing that it is.

Woolf stayed true to her own entreaty in *Three Guineas* not to succumb to the lure of prizes as a way of verifying the worth of our lives. She declined the Companion of Honour, the presidency of the writers' association PEN and honorary degrees from the universities of Liverpool and Manchester. She also turned down an invitation to give the Clark Lectures at Trinity College, Cambridge – hard as that must have been when her father had given the first Clark Lectures in 1888.

'It is an utterly corrupt society . . . and I will take nothing that it can give me,' Woolf wrote in her diary on 25 March 1933, quoting her character Elvira Pargiter. It would be awkward, she conceded, to write to the vice-chancellor of the University of Manchester refusing the title of Doctor of Letters. But it had to be done: 'Nothing would induce me to connive at all that humbug.' No false modesty led her to turn down these honours; she knew the value of her work. But she refused to be pinned down by prizes, which are meant to burnish a life and only end up diminishing it.

The second thing that people know about Woolf is that she killed herself, after a long struggle with depression. But one of the side-tragedies of suicide is that a life is then defined by a single moment – in Woolf's case, that early spring morning in 1941 when she weighted her pocket with a large stone and drowned herself in the River Ouse near Monk's House. The whole life that precedes it comes to be seen retrospectively and irrefutably as a failure. Otherwise why would its owner have thrown it away? Compounding this, in Woolf's time, was the social shame of taboo. Suicide was a criminal act.

And yet to define Woolf's life by how it ended would be a travesty. It misses so much: her many fertile, non-depressive days; the richness of her relations with her friends and family; the ferocious fun she could be, a great wit and teller of stories and laugher at other people's jokes, although you would never know it from photographs; and how droll she often was in her writing, teasing and goading the breed of men now known as mansplainers – the men whom she, the cleverest one in any room, suffered manfully all her life.

Above all it misses a central truth about Woolf's work: her constant, raw astonishment at the bare fact of being alive. To Woolf, every life – even the life of that little expiring moth – was incomparable to anything else. She would surely have agreed with Huizinga that life in its clearest and loveliest form is play – that we can't fail or succeed at it, only catch it as it flies and then let it go. If a life ends tragically, it has not 'failed'. Not if it is a life like Woolf's – a painful and difficult but also meaning-filled and matchless thing.

Spare me, then, the fake recognition of *celebrating success*. What we need most of all, more than prizes, is a sense that we have been attended to, listened to and worried about. We want our existence to be acknowledged and noted. In my life I have felt happiest not when being flattered but when being fully held in someone else's head, if only for a few moments. The best compliment you can pay someone is not to pepper them with applause emojis but to be interested in what they say and do. We just need to be noticed – or loved, which is the same thing.

When we feel fully noticed, we start to notice others fully. And then we notice something else: life itself is a celebration to which everyone is invited. All we have to do is turn up. It doesn't matter if we fail at it, because there is always enough life for everyone. Life is not a prize to be snatched at before others can get hold of it. It is the world's gift to us all, nature's bounty, as free as windfall – as long as we are ready to receive it.

So let us join that society of outsiders that Woolf urged us to join. It certainly looks more inviting than the company of those overdressed men in *Three Guineas*, freighted with gold and ermine. Outside of all that pomp and circumstance, we can be truly inside our own life, unbeholden to anyone else's belittling idea of it. Life can be hell (sometimes), but there is so much more to it than prizes.

5.

None of Us Is Proust

Or how creative failure is like life

In 2011, the artist Cory Arcangel created a bot that searched for and retweeted anyone who sent a tweet containing the words 'working on my novel'.

Many of the tweeters sounded rather pleased with themselves. Some cheerfully admitted to multitasking – to writing their novels while listening to Fleetwood Mac, drinking mimosas by the pool or waiting for their hair to set. Others assured their publics that they would be working on their novels just as soon as they came off Pinterest or were done watching *Doctor Who*. Others put a brave face on not having written for a while. But all were adamant that they were, or soon would be, working on their novels.

Arcangel later published these tweets as a book, which was funny in a queasy-making way. Despite his protests to the contrary, it felt as if these aspiring authors, mute inglorious Miltons all, were victims of a drive-by act of web-harvested ridicule. All had agreed to be in the book, but this only compounded the insult by implying that they didn't get the joke – any more than did the subjects of one of Arcangel's previous projects, 'Sorry I Haven't Posted', a collection of people apologizing for not updating their unread blogs.

I doubt many, perhaps any, of these authors finished, let alone published, their novels. But so what? Progress in writing is usually slow, absent or invisible, and these different states can look confusingly alike. However hard you cultivate your imagination, the harvest of words remains unreliable. A day's labour might yield a few salvageable sentences, or nothing. At times, writing can feel less like real work than like a selfish, neurotic tic you can't shake off – a matter of typing away futilely to no one in particular, rather as some people talk to themselves in the street while passers-by look away and quicken their pace.

Writing is a long game, a leap into the dark with uncertain outcome. Its essential adjunct is daydreaming. I find writing even a few sentences laborious, and I can only steel myself to do it by imagining readers falling on those sentences with euphoric welcome. I am in no position to mock my fellow failures for shouting to the world that they are working on their novels.

Writing inspires its own mythology of failure and atonement. These myths offer succour to the failed author with their stories of successful books that emerged out of umpteen abandoned drafts, or were rejected by every publisher but one, or got rescued from the bottom of a slush pile, or were unread when they came out and are now classics. Just because these things sometimes happen in real life doesn't stop them all being versions of the same fairy tale. The hard facts are economic. Writing is a bear market in which sellers always outnumber buyers.

I know. There is nothing more tedious than a writer telling you how hard his job is. Literary failure is no worse, and often much cushier, than other kinds of failure. It is, however, usually more conclusive. Many failures can't be easily measured, but literary failure offers a bald equation of number of hours wasted per zero words published. It has a distilled, exemplary quality that may help to illuminate that universal human feeling: failure.

Even successful authors mostly give birth to stillborn words. Literary history ignores this shadow world of the unpublished and the unreadable. Our gigantic word landfill of half-written memoirs, discarded novels and abortive poems gets bigger every year, albeit these days in virtual rather than paper form. It lives on in old memory sticks, or the hard drives of computers junked and left to die on rubbish tips, or unreadable floppy disks buried at the backs of drawers.

In any creative life, failure is more plentiful than success. There will always be more thrown-out drafts than printed books, more remaindered stock than bestsellers, more unfinished than finished paintings, more unmade film treatments than films, more songs half-written than were ever sung. Most of the world's masterpieces only happened in someone's head. The history of creativity is a long saga of misplaced effort.

You wouldn't know this, though, from the language of contemporary capitalism. *Creativity* is one of those words, like *innovation* and *empathy*, that always carries positive vibes. *Creativity* is the ingredient sprinkled on any money-making enterprise to make it feel fresh, human and palatable. The trouble with this is that capitalism's true measure of success is productivity: the rate of output per unit of input. And creativity can't be measured like that; it may even be hard to work out what its inputs and outputs are. The creative life is one of small victories interrupting long spells of frustration and disenchantment. Not so different, then, from any other life.

Early one bright May morning in 1960, a tall, shambling, round-shouldered figure went walking down London's Charing Cross Road. His name was Paul Potts and as he set off on this private mission he was in good cheer. In those days Charing Cross Road was lined with bookshops, and Potts had just had his first book of prose published after a quarter-century of trying. 'The book itself was smiling at me from the windows of the bookshops as I passed,' he wrote later, in a radio essay for the BBC Home Service. On the corner of Manette Street he stopped at Foyles, the biggest book shop on the walk (and, so it claimed, the world). And there was his book, with its striking scarlet and mustard-yellow cover, prominently displayed. In his pocket were clipped-out reviews of the book, with headlines like 'Laurel leaves at last' and 'More than one magnificence'. All this about a man who had been called for years, and on this very street, 'a useless no-good, a bum, a loafer, and a cad'.

Potts also had a letter in his pocket from his commanding officer during the war. He had been no one's idea of a soldier but had stunned those who knew him by enlisting in the Commandos. He turned out to be as useless as they had feared and ended up as an officer's batman, before being sent back to London to look after his battalion's pet dog. 'I have just read your book,' his CO's letter said. 'I wish we were still in the army, so that I could salute you.'

Potts still looked and lived like a failure. He had spent that night at the King's Cross Rowton House, one of a chain of huge red-brick hostels with hundreds of little cubicles, each containing a single bed. For five shillings you got clean sheets and a hot bath, but little else. *Len Deighton's London Dossier*, published a few years later, described the Rowton Houses as 'grim places, echoing with the cries and coughs of defeated men'.[1]

Potts had been hanging around Soho since before the war. Sleeping in bedsits and night shelters, he spent his waking hours in the pubs and cafes around Old Compton Street, and on benches reading newspapers. It was a convivial milieu for a failure, this tight lattice of low-slung streets and back alleys to the north of Shaftesbury Avenue and south of Oxford Street. Soho had become a kind of free university that broke down barriers of class, age and race. Famous writers, poets and painters mixed with gone-to-seed aristocrats, jobbing journalists, impecunious poets, stagehands and dressers at West End theatres, strippers, prostitutes and semi-retired criminals. Drinking away an afternoon in the Coach and Horses on Greek Street or the Colony Room on Dean Street meant conceding that you were a failure, or that you didn't care about success, or both.

Before becoming a failed prose writer, Potts had been a failed poet. He peddled his own wares, selling his poems as broadsheets in pubs for a penny each, under the banner headline 'A poet to his people'. After he published a slim volume of these poems called *Instead of a Sonnet*, the Soho poet David Wright wrote an 'appreciation' of Potts in *Poetry Quarterly* entitled 'Instead of a poet'. Potts's poems were, he wrote, 'technically the worst verse ever written by a poet, but much preferable to the polished masturbations of some versifiers'. Wright went on to praise Potts's prose, but added that 'it is, fortunately, some years since he last wrote any verses'. Potts concurred with this view, writing in the preface to *Instead of a Sonnet*: 'To read my verse is to share my failure; it is but the weakling harvest of an exciting spring.'[2]

Potts had an air of gloom about him and seemed to invite misfortune. Some time in the late 1940s the poet Laurie Lee, from his attic flat in a Chelsea square, shot at Potts on the pavement below with an air rifle, just because he thought 'there were too many poets around'. According to Lee, when the pellet landed on Potts's foot he turned round, rebuked the blameless woman behind him and then 'left immediately for the Hebrides'.[3] This must have been to see his friend George Orwell on Jura. Orwell seems at least to have tolerated Potts, but Orwell's friends, and his sister Avril, found him insufferable.

Now, with many unpublished books behind him, he had published *Dante Called You Beatrice*. This book about failure had been, quite unforeseeably, a semi-success, even being chosen as a Readers' Union book club selection. The reviews were not quite as gushing as Potts claimed. In the *Evening Standard*, Michael Foot said the book had 'the suggestion of greatness'. In the *Times Literary Supplement*, Alan Ross called it 'a touching, warm, aphoristic, formless book . . . in which fine phrases lie side by side with sentences of astonishing silliness and triteness'. In the

Listener, Stephen Spender judged it 'a disturbing, sympathetic, though, at times, exasperating book . . . a few yards cut off the tape recording of an endless monologue'.[4] Oh, well. A writer is permitted to edit his reviews.

But now that the book existed, Potts confessed to a sense of deflation. The launch of a book leaves an author in little doubt about the disparity between its dreamt-of and its actual impact. A thing nursed lovingly for years in the shadows can seem dull and leaden in the light of day. 'One's dreams do really look very big inside one's loneliness, because quite simply there is very often nothing else there at all,' he told listeners in that radio essay. Now that something he had carried inside his head for years had set out on a life of its own, it was bound to look mean and shrivelled when forced to exist in the unforgiving world. 'In a way,' he said, 'I had never felt such a failure before in my life.'[5]

A month after Paul Potts walked down Charing Cross Road, another Soho regular had a far more spectacular success, a few hundred yards away in St Martin's Lane. Lionel Bart was part of a younger Soho, milling around the new espresso and milk bars on Old Compton Street. He did not have to wait as long as Potts for his great moment, which arrived just before his thirtieth birthday.

On 30 June 1960, in the middle of a heatwave, *Oliver!* opened at the New Theatre. For a musical, the subject matter was dark: street gangs, crime, prostitution, death. But Bart's songs were thrillingly alive, an anarchic melding of Jewish klezmer music, Broadway torch songs, music-hall oompah-pah and Tin Pan Alley pop. Unable to read music, he composed them by singing tunes into a tape recorder. He claimed never to spend more than an hour on a song, believing they should be as spontaneous as sneezes. And yet they ended up just the right mix of familiar and fresh, of hooky melodies and startling tritones.

The first-night audience gently applauded the opening numbers. Then halfway through the first act, at the end of 'Consider Yourself', they went wild. The set revolved for the next scene, in Fagin's den, but Ron Moody, as Fagin, had to wait several minutes until the audience calmed down. At the end of the show there were twenty-three curtain calls and many reprises of 'Consider Yourself' and 'I'd Do Anything' before Bart was called on stage with cries of 'Author! Author!' For most of us, this kind of life-defining affirmation occurs only in our most self-indulgent daydreams. Ron Moody felt 'a kind of electrical magnetism around the theatre. I've never known it since. It's something called success.'[6] *Oliver!* went on to run in the West End for six years.

Thus began what Bart later called 'my flash git period'. He became the richest person in showbiz in Britain – until overtaken by his friends, the Beatles. His Chelsea mansion, in a cul-de-sac off the Fulham Road, was all mock-baronial Gothic and bachelor-pad, push-button modernity. It had a sunken bath, a full-sized cinema, a Gothic hall with two huge chandeliers, a sauna and a bathroom with a high-backed, dark-wooden, ecclesiastical-looking toilet and a toilet-paper holder that played Handel's water music. Here he held parties and kept open house. On the coffee tables were piles of marijuana and bowls stuffed with ten-pound notes for guests to help themselves. Bart was one of seven surviving children born to Jewish refugees from Austria–Hungary and brought up in poverty in London's East End. Eager to erase memories of his upbringing, he had turned himself into a stage caricature of success, as starkly drawn as the Artful Dodger.

'We live, we thrive – you keep us all alive, with "bravo!" and "bravissimo!", we're dead if it's *pianissimo*.' Ira Gershwin's song 'Applause, Applause' is one of many numbers in musical theatre asking the audience to show their appreciation of the company.

These songs remind us that cueing up applause is always a subtle act of strong-arming. We applaud as much out of duty as any sense that we are handing out a deserved reward.

The ancient Greek dramatists wrote their plays for theatrical competitions called Dionysia, at which organized cadres of applauders tried to sway the judges. In ancient Rome, plays ended with the line 'Vos valete, et plaudite, cives': 'Farewell, citizens, and we hope you are pleased.' At this prompt the audience would clap their hands, snap their fingers or wave the flap of their togas. This applause-generating convention worked its way into the epilogues of early modern comedies. *A Midsummer Night's Dream* ends with Puck's 'Give me your hands, if we be friends, / And Robin shall restore amends.' *Volpone* ends with 'The seasoning of a play is the applause.'

On the Regency London stage, a *claptrap* was a trick to catch applause with cheap sentiment – from which comes the modern sense of the word as rubbish or nonsense. Nineteenth-century theatre and opera relied on the *claque*, a group of hired applauders (from the French *claquer*, to slap). Parisian theatres employed different types of *claqueur* such as *bisseurs* (demanding *bis*, or encore), *pleureuses* (crying at sad moments) and *rieurs* (laughing on cue). The *chef de claque*, or chief clapper, would attend rehearsals, work out the optimum moments for applause and direct the *claqueurs* accordingly.

As a boy, I watched a TV talent show called *Opportunity Knocks*. At the end of each show the competing acts gave a short reprise of their routine while the studio audience applauded. The applause was measured, up to a hundred, on a rickety piece of supposed technical wizardry called a clapometer. The clapometer was 'just for fun, friends', as the host, Hughie Green, reminded viewers each week. It declared only the studio winner – what really counted were the viewers' votes, sent in by postcard. But the clapometer entered national myth as the will of the people enshrined. Parents told their children that if they clapped in their living room it would show up on the clapometer. I found all this puzzling. How can you measure applause, and why would you want to?

My further education in the oddness of applause came in sixth form. We went as a class to form part of the studio audience for a television game show called *The Krypton Factor*. Before filming began, the floor manager taught us how to make the sound of two people clapping. Instead of clapping near our laps, we had to raise our hands near our heads and clap from there, at twice normal speed. At the end of each segment he would run to the front of the audience and applaud agitatedly in double time above his head, urging us to do the same. After a while – and with all the interruptions and retakes, a half-hour programme ended up lasting over two hours – my arms ached and my palms stung. It was exhausting. It made me wonder about the point of applause that must be so commanded to appear.

In my office at work, I often hear, emanating from some nearby classroom, tiny smatterings of applause. Someone has finished a presentation and the audience is acknowledging them in the customary way. No more than a dozen pairs of hands by the sound of it, working in well-mannered unison. Sometimes the clapping begins just as I have come to the end of some menial task. For a microsecond I imagine I am being applauded for closing my filing cabinet, or pressing send on an email, or successfully aiming a wodge of paper at the wastepaper basket. Strange things to be applauded for, but then all applause is strange.

In his book *Cool Memories*, Jean Baudrillard notes that 'nothing can match the loneliness of a pianist in a large hotel'. All around him is the hum of conversation and clink of cocktail glasses; everyone ignores the ambient tinkling of the keys on his piano. When he stops playing, people applaud, but he knows that this is only because the music has fallen silent, a silence the crowd notices 'in much the same way they notice the sugar melting in their glasses'.[7] Most applause is a polite reflex. It is meant to signal collective approval at something successfully done, but those who receive it know in their hearts that it is just a nod to courtesy and custom.

Applause in musical theatre is more clarifying. It strips away all this polite inscrutability and leaves no one in doubt what we are witnessing: a smash or a flop. Singers in musicals learn how to billboard a line, creating a crescendo to cue a clap. Numbers end with a stinger: a staccato, unison note, like a hard full stop. The stinger is designed to deliver applause as the bell delivered saliva into the mouths of Pavlov's dogs. If it works, as with 'Consider Yourself', it stops the show. If it fails, it fails utterly.

John Osborne's musical *The World of Paul Slickey* opened at the Palace Theatre in May 1959. The *Evening Standard* critic Milton Shulman wrote that the first-night audience was 'about equally divided between those who loathed it politely and those who hated it audibly'. Noël Coward wrote in his diary late that night: 'Never in all my theatrical experience have I seen anything so appalling . . . Bad lyrics, dull music, idiotic, would-be-daring dialogue – interminable long-winded scenes about nothing, and above all the amateurishness and ineptitude, such bad taste that one wanted to hide one's head.'[8]

Osborne, who had given a two-fingered salute to the gallery at the end, was booed as he came out of the theatre by a small crowd shouting 'Tripe!' and 'Bloody rubbish!' Some of this unhappy group followed him up Charing Cross Road until he escaped into a taxi. 'I must be the only playwright this century,' he wrote later, 'to have been pursued up a London street by an angry mob.'[9] By the end of the show's six-week run the cast were placing bets on when the audience would start booing.

As its title suggests, *Dante Called You Beatrice* is about Paul Potts's long, unrequited love for an unnamed woman. But it is also about the failed career of a writer who has 'found pawnbrokers much kinder than editors'. Potts describes himself, at forty-eight, as 'a man who owns nothing, one who has accomplished nothing . . . A poet with no poems, a writer with no books.' Gradually he overlays his theme of unrequited love with another, related one: writing itself as a kind of unrequited love, and similarly debasing. 'I have tried,' Potts writes, 'to make the English language fall in love with the thinking in my heart.'

In its fusion of literary sociology and earnest confession, the book is clearly conceived as another *Enemies of Promise* or *The Unquiet Grave* – Cyril Connolly's classic works about frustrated writerly ambition. Like Connolly, Potts cultivates the persona of a genius manqué, destroyed by melancholy and perfectionism. But Cyril Connolly he isn't. *Dante Called You Beatrice* is by turns touching, astute, querulous, repetitive and absent of any trace of humour. In describing one of his failed projects, Potts also manages to describe *Dante Called You Beatrice* quite well: 'It wasn't a book at all really, it was just some writing as long as a book.'

Still, Potts happened to have a good ear for sentences, in the same way that some singers happen to have a pleasing timbre. And he put this good ear to use in dissecting and anatomizing his own failure. 'I believed, I loved and I fumbled,' he writes. 'I had the ball right in front of the goal post, when I suddenly got cramp, the goal post disappeared and the ball rolled away.' Shrewd enough to concede that in his benighted century he has led a cosier life than most, he is also honest enough to say that failure is no less real for being relative. 'Compared to the taste I had in my mouth before I sat down,' he writes, 'the meal to say the least of it, was rather thin.'[10]

The book's big flaw is that Potts, like many self-defining failures, is too uninhibited. He has no friends to alienate, no reputation to uphold, no achievements to preserve, no end to keep up. So he spews up all his undigested umbrage on to the page. Like the Ancient Mariner, Potts occasionally waylays his listener with salient news from the country of failure. Self-pity is a potent and universal feeling, and on the other side of it may be found wisdom. But by its nature it is an antisocial pursuit. Like alcohol, it is best drunk in moderation, when it offers temporary solace, and not to excess, when it only makes us feel worse. A wise author conceals it or at least dials it down. Trying to elicit sympathy for decades of failure, as Potts does in his book, is itself a failure, of tact and tone. Why should the reader care? They don't know the writer and owe him nothing, not even the obligation to read on. No one ever succeeded in making self-pity endearing.

After *Oliver!*, Lionel Bart wrote two minor hit musicals, *Maggie May* and *Blitz*, but craved another smash. So he poured all his efforts into a new project, a spoof on the legend of Robin Hood. To go one better than *Oliver!*, he gave its title two exclamation marks. *Twang!!* became one of the most famous failures in musical theatre history.

Even before it opened, the newspapers were reporting fraught rehearsals and backstage feuds. The radical theatre impresario Joan Littlewood had been made director, despite having hated *Oliver!* and walked out of both *Blitz* and *Maggie May* during the interval. Her method, honed at her company Theatre Workshop, was to take the script apart and improvise wildly before pulling the whole production together at the last minute. She spent rehearsals getting the cast to mime dying trees, perform ad-lib operas or pretend to be Vietcong fighting the Americans. Bart attended the rehearsals and threw in ideas, one of which was that Robin Hood should enter on a forklift truck.

The show's pre-London premiere, at Manchester's Palace Theatre, was a disaster. The improvised dialogue fell flat. The jokes were met with silence. The book was confusing. The scenes bore no relation to the unmemorable songs. And at three-and-a-half hours it all went on far too long. The set design of Sherwood Forest was a small triumph – but, as they say in the business, audiences don't come out humming the set. The day before press night, Littlewood resigned. One of the producers said that bringing the show to London would be 'like giving a crazy man £30,000 and having him flush the notes down the toilet one by one'.[11]

Twang!! opened at the Shaftesbury Theatre a few days before Christmas. Bart had financed the London run himself by signing away a half-share in the profits of all his future music publishing for the next decade. The performers were by now exhausted, from having to learn new lines and songs while still performing each night. The words they had no time to learn were taped on to the back of the scenery. None of the changes worked. R. B. Marriott in the *Stage* judged it 'a dank, bedraggled, feeble thing'. Jeremy Rundall in *Plays and Players* thought 'it really has no business on a professional stage before a paying audience'. *The Times* called it 'a show without a single witty line, a single memorable song, or a single arresting situation'.[12]

The same *Times* critic also pondered: 'There is often something mystifying in the way that musicals swallow up prodigious investments in money and yield nothing in return.' This was an understatement. Musicals swallow up not just money but large chunks of people's egos, their energies and their lives, and yield in return something far worse than nothing: failure, ridicule, ruin.

The closing notice for *Twang!!* went up on 14 January. Littlewood's replacement as director, Burt Shevelove, posted some parting words to the company on the stage door: 'We all stood on tiptoe, for a long time, and nobody gave us a kiss.'[13] The musical flop is an even more lowering act of unrequited love than a failed book – because the rejection is unequivocal and it happens in public.

Stories of musical flops elicit a special kind of schadenfreude on account of the gaping disparity between ambition and achievement. A flop involves no less an investment of time and energy than a hit. The strange alchemy of success either happens or not; the soufflé rises or it doesn't. The musical *Kelly*, about a man who kills himself by jumping off the Brooklyn Bridge ('a bad idea gone wrong' – *Herald Tribune*), closed on its opening night on Broadway in 1965. *Home Sweet Homer*, starring Yul Brynner as Odysseus – 'one of the dumbest musicals in Broadway history' according to the historian of musical flops Ken Mandelbaum[14] – opened and closed on a single Sunday matinee in 1976. *Oscar Wilde*, a musical written by a former BBC Radio 1 DJ, Mike Read, closed after its opening night at the Shaw Theatre in London in 2004, having sold only five tickets for the next performance.

The gruesome fascination with such failure derives not only from its abjectness but from the cavernous gap between simulated joy and actual misery. A musical feeds off forced vivacity and bogus good cheer. The performers, with their perma-smiles and jazz hands flung wide at the end of each routine, are needily asking for love. Musicals require such investments of time and money that their being loved is both an emotional and financial imperative. The audience, even if they know they are being worked on by those melodic tugs and orchestral swells, may decide to play along. Or they may find it harder to love something that is trying so hard to be loved.

Musical theatre's greatest asset is also its greatest weakness: a pathetic eagerness to please. Onstage is all fatuous, affected joie de vivre; offstage is all panicked rewrites, fights, tears, walkouts and lawsuits. Larry Gelbart, before he co-wrote *A Funny Thing Happened on the Way to the Forum*, wrote a flop, *The Conquering Hero*. Its ill-starred off-Broadway run in 1961 inspired his rueful line: 'If Hitler is alive, I hope he's out of town with a musical.'[15]

Every economist knows of the sunk cost fallacy – otherwise known as pouring good money after bad. In an article in *Nature* in 1976, Richard Dawkins and Tamsin Carlisle gave this phenomenon another name: the Concorde fallacy. British and French governments continued to invest in the Concorde supersonic airliner long after it became uneconomical, because they were anxious to justify the huge joint investment they had already made.

Dawkins and Carlisle argued that only humans would be this irrational – that, following the logic of natural selection, other animals would come to more optimal decisions. But Dawkins went on to do research with Jane Brockmann on the female great golden digger wasp, and they found that wasps were just as susceptible to the Concorde fallacy. The female digger wasp digs a burrow where she keeps all the katydids she has caught and paralysed to feed her young. She digs her burrow close to where she herself hatched, and so nesting areas start to form. This means that a wasp often comes across a burrow that another wasp has dug, and occupies it rather than face digging her own.

Sometimes a squatter wasp meets a previous-owner wasp at the entrance to the burrow, and they fight over it until the loser flees. Brockmann and Dawkins found that the amount of time a wasp will fight over a disputed nest depends not on how many katydids are in there but on how many she herself has put in there. This is illogical. She has no rational reason to defend the nest more tenaciously because of the work she has already done; only the nest's current value to her should matter. But she is, as we also say of humans, overinvested.[16]

Sunk costs are irrecoverable and should by rights be discounted in subsequent decisions. But people cannot help taking unconscious account of them and continuing to invest in obviously failing ventures. We carry on thinking that we can escape from our gambling debts with one last punt or that we should keep eating a disgusting meal because we have already paid for it. Wounded pride and unwillingness to face the shame of failure play their part. Economists call it 'escalation of commitment'.

Musical flops feed this kind of fallacy all the time. About his own experience of a flop, John Osborne wrote that those involved in musicals are gripped by a 'myopic faith'.[17] They persist in their belief that the problems are only technical and that minor adjustments will solve everything. Maybe they take heart from the plot of so many musicals, where everything comes good on opening night after the unknown chorus girl is plucked from the line when the star gets sick.

Faith turns to denial, then delusion. A musical ignoramus could tell from its first chords that *Twang!!* was a dud. Everyone could hear, see and even smell it – that whiff of defeat coming from the stage. Everyone, that is, except the digger-wasp composer who was thinking about all the work he had put into it and how he could still make it a hit.

Paul Potts suffered from his own version of the sunk cost fallacy. Unlike Bart, he did not throw away thousands of pounds of his own money – only his whole life. He made the mistake many writers make, of thinking that writing one little masterpiece would make everything all right. 'One work of art, if I could but make one, one book, one poem, even one really great sentence, would put me beyond the reach of the literary spivs for ever,' he wrote. 'Then all the shabby shame of not being able to do something properly would be cleared away.'[18] It wouldn't and it wasn't. *Dante Called You Beatrice* was soon forgotten. The nearest it came to immortality was being chosen, briefly and implausibly, as an A-level set text. Potts did not find this out until much later and resented not being told.

A writer can't perform the equivalent of a stinger in musical theatre, summoning up applause with just words on a page. A book can only be truly successful when its success is not its raison d'être. Its proper purpose is to be itself – something that needed to exist more than its author needed to be loved. A book only works if it feels like a gift to the world, and a gift can't be given with provisos or the prospect of reward. For a writer to admit to disappointment that his gift was not as rapturously received as he would have wished is a breach of etiquette, as unseemly as demanding that unrequited love be returned.

Potts kept on writing, and a small helping of his words even got published. But nothing came close to the very modest success of *Dante Called You Beatrice*. His writings became ever more cantankerous and chaotically arranged. With his last published book, *Invitation to a Sacrament*, self-pity got the better of syntax. His comma-spliced, broken-backed sentences, some of which recycle lines from his earlier work, forget their beginning before they have reached their end. 'Take your laurel leaves away,' goes one of them, 'neither do I like the smell of myrtle, you come and bring praise now while the sun is out you bring your lamps, but where were you the night they threw me into Pentonville, when hungry I could never find you.'[19]

'A work like this does not need a blurb,' the dustjacket copy from his clearly nonplussed publishers, Martin Brian and O'Keeffe, insisted. *Invitation to a Sacrament* is poetry, the blurb went on, 'such real poetry that it does not need the verse, which is just as well, as his verse is terrible'. It ended with a shoulder shrug: 'Read it for yourself and find out.'

Potts's shuffling figure was still a familiar sight in Soho. He was by now mainly renowned for tapping people for money and for his offensive body odour. He would complain to anyone who would buy him a Guinness that he should have become a doctor or an architect instead of living in dosshouses scraping a non-living. He cadged review copies of books from the offices of weekly magazines and sold them straight to the second-hand bookshops on Charing Cross Road. He dined in Soho restaurants and walked out without paying, leaving nearby acquaintances to settle the bill. He had a habit of kicking those who displeased him – male and female – in the shins.

Potts also pilfered concealable items, such as shirts and ashtrays, when he visited people's homes. He once stole a Corona typewriter from Iris Murdoch because, he said, he needed it more than she did. The Soho writer Jeffrey Bernard accused Potts of stealing a silk tie from him and then having the effrontery to wear it when they met in the pub the next day. He once saw Potts stop dead in the street, gaze skywards and scream.

In 1986, Potts, now seventy-five, had his photograph taken for Christopher and Sebastian Barker's book *Portraits of Poets*. By then he was barely a poet at all, so it should have been an honour to be photographed alongside Ted Hughes, John Betjeman, Philip Larkin and Elizabeth Jennings. Instead it looked more like an unmasking. Sat on the bed in his Highbury flat, Potts tilts his head, with its bald dome, unkempt side-hair and tramp's beard, and looks forlornly at the camera. He is wearing a donkey jacket and a blanket over his lower half, one of his huge, grubby hands not quite resting on a walking stick. Behind him, the peeling wallpaper is fighting a losing battle with mould.

Jeffrey Bernard was a far more successful failure than Paul Potts. He summed up his own failed life in a spoof obituary he wrote in 1978. He first visited Soho aged fourteen in 1946, it began, 'and from that point he was never to look forward'. Here in the cafes and pubs of Dean Street and Old Compton Street he developed 'his remarkable sloth, envy and self-pity'. He spent so much time drinking and gambling on horses that he was unable to hold down an ordinary job and 'was consequently advised to take up journalism'.[20] The obituary appeared in Bernard's weekly 'Low Life' column in the *Spectator*. Here, for twenty-one years, he chronicled a life spent propping up bars and observing his own physical decline.

Sometimes, as he spent longer spells in the alcoholic ward at Middlesex Hospital, the *Spectator* announced, at the bottom of a column written by a substitute, 'Jeffrey Bernard is unwell.' In

1989, Keith Waterhouse used this line as the title of a hit West End play based on Bernard's life, starring Peter O'Toole. The show turned Bernard into a public figure. Strangers pointed him out in the bar of the Apollo Theatre on Shaftesbury Avenue, where he sat during the show. Or they loitered in the Coach and Horses, hoping to buy him a large vodka and soda. Even though Bernard had never written the autobiography that publishers had long invited him to undertake, even though he had failed to write many other books for which he had spent the advances, even though his right leg had to be amputated below the knee after gangrene set in, he was now a success – his reputation owing entirely to a column about wasting his life.

Bernard's writing was sandpaper-charming and mordantly funny. It smoothly conveyed the Soho creed that success in the world beyond that small grid of streets in London W1D was irretrievably infra dig. If drinking one's life away in an unending series of dead afternoons made you a failure, it was still nobler than slapping backs and air-kissing cheeks 'in a common, vulgar Park Lane hotel collecting awards that look like bronze Henry Moore turds'.[21] Yet Bernard's columns make for painful reading today. They are full of homophobia (Soho: ruined by gays), casual racism (London: overrun by Arabs), standard-issue misogyny (women: money-grubbing 'birds' or middle-aged 'boilers') and a pervading, barely concealed sourness.

Bernard was no more likeable than Potts, but he had followed to the letter two unwritten Soho rules of which Potts fell foul. If you fail, you can't be a bore about it; if you succeed, ditto, and you must also dilute it with self-destructiveness. These unwritten rules made Bernard rich in Soho's real, non-convertible currency, respect. He carried on writing his column until a fortnight before his death, tinder-dry funny to the end – although he now wrote about being so weak that he could barely get out of the bath and about whether he should effectively end his own life by refusing dialysis (which he did). Even at the sharp end of failure a hierarchy remains; some just carry it off better than others.

Lionel Bart's failure was the most theatrical, because he had furthest to fall. *Twang!!* virtually ended his career. His musical version of Fellini's film *La Strada* ran for just one performance on Broadway in December 1969, by which time it had been stripped of all but three of his songs. He wrote other musicals – based on *Gulliver's Travels*, *The Hunchback of Notre Dame*, *Cyrano de Bergerac* and the life of Golda Meir – but none were performed. He also sold the rights to *Oliver!*, losing him millions in royalties. In 1972, he filed for bankruptcy, with six-figure debts and assets of only £624. By now he was both an alcoholic and a drug addict, prone to what he called 'ostriches' – shutting himself away on his own for days at a time.

At first glance, Bart's decline reads like a morality tale. Hubris inspires nemesis; prodigality and overreach bring bankruptcy and disgrace. But this obscures a simpler truth: failure in musical theatre, just as in life, is routine. In musicals, also as in life, things fail for lots of reasons. Unpacking all the variables and isolating a central cause is as irresolvable as in chaos theory. A hit musical is a near-impossible trick to pull off. In the journey from idea to opening night, so many different egos, skills and talents need to come together that failure is by far the likeliest end.

Musicals are innately silly, full of awkward artifice and surreal juxtapositions. In real life, people do not suddenly burst into full-throated song, dancing manically around each other as if it were the most normal thing in the world, before resuming their conversation as if nothing has happened. This in-built absurdity scuppers any formula for either success or failure.

Plenty of hit musicals have emerged out of preposterous premises that on paper doomed them to fail. An Irishman steals a crock of gold from a leprechaun and comes to plant it in America, where his daughter gets involved in a sharecropper revolt against a bigoted senator, who sees the error of his ways when he temporarily becomes black (*Finian's Rainbow*). A tribe of cats come together at a ball to decide which cat will ascend to cat heaven (*Cats*). An obsolete steam engine races against modern engines, the trains played by performers on roller skates running on tracks around the auditorium (*Starlight Express*). In musical theatre there is no such thing as a sure-fire flop – a truth that drives the plot of Mel Brooks's film *The Producers*, later a hit musical.

Musicals tread a line as thin as a toddler's shoe between the exultant and the ludicrous. There is something life-affirming about their readiness to fling their arms wide, hoping against hope for the world's embrace. As their creators strive to build something madly beautiful out of words, music and movement, even they know that it will probably just make them look desperate and daft.

So why do it? Perhaps because to make something madly beautiful you have to risk making something execrable. The same misled tenacity that makes us fall on our faces also takes us to the greatest heights. And when it comes off – linking into an unbroken whole all these competing elements of song, lyric, dance, dialogue and story – it is just so wondrously unlikely that the whole world cheers. The most magnificent artistic success flies closest to the flames of failure. As Saphir says in Gilbert and Sullivan's *Patience*: 'Nonsense, yes, perhaps – but oh, what precious nonsense!'

To all but a few surviving regulars of old Soho, the name 'Paul Potts' now evokes only the operatic tenor who won the first series of *Britain's Got Talent*. The film *One Chance*, starring James Corden, tells his story. Its plot – a socially awkward hero survives childhood bullying, a disapproving dad and a job as a mobile phone salesman to become a famous singer who makes grown men weep – traces the standard feelgood curve. The other Paul Potts has been forgotten.

But that word *forgotten* is so often used to pass a subtle kind of judgement, reducing the forgotten thing to a sad irrelevance. *A long-forgotten book. A now-forgotten author.* But who is it doing the forgetting? Us. The forgotten person is hardly to blame because, inside our little bubble of presentist self-concern, we can't be bothered to remember them and have forgotten that we will also be forgotten. Is any past life a failure just because it no longer speaks to our solipsistic concerns? We all suffer to varying degrees from this condescension towards the past, the illusion that we will escape the oblivion of our forebears. Much mental harm is done, both to themselves and others, by those obsessed with their legacy and the judgement of posterity. History teaches us humility. If failure means being forgotten, then everyone fails in the end.

In a former life, I was a historian of the everyday. It meant spending a lot of time reading old newspapers, making many trips up the Northern line to the now-defunct British Newspaper Library at Colindale, with its special smell of crumbling old paper and printers' ink. Looking through old newspapers always felt mildly subversive, because they were not designed to be read after the date on their masthead. The French for newspaper – *journal*, or 'of the day' – sums it up. The Greek is *efimerida*: a piece of ephemera. Like the ephemeron fly, the newspaper is meant to die on the day it is born. Old newspapers have been used, within recent memory, for fish-and-chip wrapping and bottom-wiping.

Scrolling through thousands of pages of the *Daily Sketch* or the *News Chronicle* in the Colindale microfilm room brought home to me the disposability of all writing, and of all our attempts to record human life as it slips away. Reading the arts reviews and listings in old newspapers felt like entering a lost world of spent effort. It made me see what a sieve-like vessel our collective memory is and how many celebrated people are forgotten long before their lives are over – 'Runners whom renown outran / And the name died before the man,' in A. E. Housman's words.

'In the long run we are all dead,' the novelist Anne Enright writes, 'and none of us is Proust.' Even successful authors see themselves as failures. Chekhov complained in his letters about railway bookstores not stocking his books. Henry James was a failed playwright, William Faulkner a failed poet. Paul Potts's friend George Orwell saw his career as mostly wasted time and wrote in his essay 'Why I Write' that 'every book is a failure'. When T. S. Eliot's publisher, Robert Giroux, suggested to him that most editors are failed writers, he replied: 'Perhaps, but so are most writers.' Ezra Pound, interviewed by Allen Ginsberg near the end of his life, called his own work 'a mess . . . stupidity and ignorance all the way through . . . I found out after seventy years I was not a lunatic but a moron.' When Philip Roth gave up writing aged eighty, unable any more to stand the daily frustration, he said: 'It's just like baseball: you fail two-thirds of the time.'

Writing appears to be exempt from the 10,000 hours rule – that theory, with its suspiciously round number, which contends that the key to achieving expertise in any field is to practise the right way for long enough. In writing, no amount of work imparts mastery. Nor does worldly success offer indemnity against what Zadie Smith has called the 'intimate side of literary failure', the ways in which writers fail on their own private and singular terms. Smith imagines this land of literary failure as 'mostly beach, with hopeful writers standing on the shoreline while their perfect novels pile up, over on the opposite coast, out of reach'.

A book's publication is often a comedown, as Paul Potts intuited on that ultimately dispiriting walk down Charing Cross Road in May 1960. We invest too much in that crowning moment when we will at last have our words eternalized on thin slivers of wood pulp, glued together and enclosed in hard covers. It is sad to think of Potts so craving that moment for all those years. All that remains of that dream now is the odd copy of *Dante Called You Beatrice* soaking up the damp in a second-hand bookshop and a single one in the British Library, called up from the vaults sixty years on by another obscure writer studying failure.

Any life is a more enthralling work of art than almost any book. Take, for instance, the life of Joe Gould. The *New Yorker* writer Joseph Mitchell first wrote about Gould in 1942 in a piece titled 'Professor Sea Gull'. The similarities between Gould and Potts are striking. Gould, too, was a spiky semi-destitute who lived in fleapit hotels and flophouses, cadged loose change for his meals, stole small items from his friends and hung round the bars and cafes of a bohemian quarter, in his case Greenwich Village. Unlike Potts, though, he had a knack of making clever people consider him a genius.

For Gould was writing the world's longest book – an oral history of the ordinary people of America that was shaping up to be the seminal statement on his times. This book was going to do for modern America what Edward Gibbon did for the Roman Empire. He had begun writing it in 1917, six years after being kicked out of Harvard, scribbling it in dime-store composition books with a fountain pen filled from post-office inkstands. The book was scattered all over the city, in notebooks stored in the attics and basements of well-wishers. By the time Mitchell met him, Gould had written nine million words.

In 1964, seven years after Gould died in a mental asylum, Mitchell updated the story in another *New Yorker* piece, 'Joe Gould's Secret'. He had kept trying to set Gould up with New York editors, but his subject refused to be helped, skipping the appointments or refusing to relinquish his notebooks. Finally Mitchell got it: the book did not exist.

At first he felt played. But then he remembered that, as a young man, he had himself conceived a huge New York novel on the scale of Joyce's *Ulysses*. He could write whole chunks of it in his head in the course of a subway ride, and daydreamed hourly about the finished book, with its green and gold cover. Not a word of it was ever written. He now wondered if, given 'the Niagaras of books' pouring off the world's presses, most of them pedestrian, he and Gould had done the world a service in not giving birth to theirs.[22]

Mitchell came to see Gould as a more compelling character than could be found in most novels. He could mimic a seagull's caws and translate them into human. He could dance a Chippewa Indian stomp. And he could perform with method-acting conviction the role of the eccentric author of a great, unpublished work. He had inspired E. E. Cummings, Ezra Pound and William Saroyan to write about him, Joseph Stella and Alice Neel to paint him and Aaron Siskind to photograph him. Gould's book was probably not as chimerical as Mitchell, ever in search of a better story, made out; most likely it existed as a short and unruly pile of notes. But Gould was certainly a failure, and one in whom Mitchell found an unlikely kinship. 'Joe Gould's Secret' was Mitchell's last major work. For the next thirty-two years, until his death in 1996, he kept going into his office at the *New Yorker* but published next to nothing. One of his failed projects was writing the unwritten novel he alluded to in 'Joe Gould's Secret'.

'Because the poetry I wanted to write has not been written at all,' Potts wrote in *Dante Called You Beatrice*, 'English literature has missed a footnote. There is a little piece of truth that has not been told, a little bit of love that has not been declared.'[23] Perhaps. But perhaps the opposite is true and Potts would have been better off not publishing anything at all.

In the harsh light of posterity, distinguishing between a very slim and a non-existent oeuvre can feel like the narcissism of minor differences. What really mattered about Potts was not his writing, which was mediocre, but the work of genius that was himself. Like Joe Gould in Greenwich Village, he was a piece of

Soho street art, a walking installation on the theme of failed promise. In its own way, like Gould's, his life spawned its legends and made its mark. The great Soho photographer John Deakin took his picture. The sculptor Barry Flanagan sculpted his head in bronze. Patrick Kavanagh and W. S. Graham both name-checked him in poems. And today he turns up in strange two-sentence cameos in the biographies of more famous writers like George Orwell, Dylan Thomas and Hugh Mac-Diarmid. This is more than most of us leave behind.

It would be fitting, I think, for Paul Potts to have a memorial floor stone or wall tablet in Poet's Corner at Westminster Abbey, along with Keats, Shelley and the rest. He could be remembered as the patron saint of failed writers – standing in for us all, a bit like the unknown soldier whose tomb also lies in the Abbey. Like many writers, he could be cussed, cranky and naive about his place in the human ecosystem. But who said writers, or failures, had to be nice? And which writer has not made the same mistake that Potts made – betting the farm on the far future, when the consummation of our talents will give meaning to our lives and absolve us of our sins?

Not much solace on hand in how these stories end, I'm afraid. Potts died in 1990, alone and bedridden, burning himself alive after setting light to the bed with his pipe. Bart died nine years later, living in much reduced circumstances in a flat above a parade of shops in Acton. Buoyed a little by a winning revival of *Oliver!* at the London Palladium in 1994, he still felt underrated and unfulfilled. His only commission in his last decade was a television commercial for the Abbey National Building Society. He had, at least, convinced himself to stop drinking – after falling asleep next to his front door and being woken by the late morning post falling on his face. By then, though, it had made him diabetic and destroyed half his liver.

But still I cannot think of Bart's life as a failure – nor Paul

Potts's either. As someone who needs salaried work, with its emptying in-tray and emailed meeting reminders, to moor my life, I admire the hustling, all-or-nothing existence of the true artist. It feels as brave to me as jumping out of a plane and somehow hoping to acquire a parachute on the way down. Wanting a thing so much, and screwing up one's whole life in failing to get it, should count for *something*, shouldn't it? As Walt Whitman wrote, battles are lost in the same spirit in which they are won. Or perhaps Paul Potts put it better: 'The only difference between me and a real artist is that I am not one.'[24]

Maybe your own life has failed like a musical flop. You began it with big dreams: your name in lights, white-tie-and-tiara openings, standing ovations, cries of 'Author! Author!' Instead you end up touring out of town, staying in cheap hotels, hoping for a West End run that never materializes. You fall out with your life collaborators, pull off midnight rewrites, cut scenes and tape new lines on to the back of the scenery. You know in your heart that it isn't working and will never work, but the show must go on. Being a pro means persevering with failure. The audience rewards you with heckles and taunts, or tame applause, and the closing notice goes up long before you wanted it to. That's showbiz.

Or maybe your life is a slower-burning failure – like a book that has lived in your head for years. The journey of that book, that life, is like the course of a river from its headwaters to the sea. The idea for it begins like a spring or trickling stream. Water flows fastest near its source, so the upper course is full of excitement, with lots of rapids and waterfalls. Then the river slows down and widens into its middle age. Eventually it becomes tidal and the words lose all momentum. It is all the writer can do to keep going. But worse is to come when the river empties itself into an endless ocean made up of other people's indifference. Some might prefer a baying mob to this colder reality of silence and apathy.

You dreamt of making something enduring out of the half-formed fancies in your head, and you made this thin, watery, insipid, unregarded thing instead. It wasn't the magnum opus you conjured up in your dreams, but nothing ever is when it takes shape in the real world. It didn't get the love you had hoped for, but there is never enough love to go round. It will soon be forgotten, but so, in time, is everything else. Your failure was like billions of other failures, except that it was yours. And like those billions of other failures – all of them proof of this unquenchable desire to make a mark, to leave one's own little sketch of a woolly mammoth on the wall of a cave – it was a heroic and heartening thing.

Nor can we ever second-guess what effect our work, or the work of art that is ourselves, will have on others. Writing, Rebecca Solnit argues, is 'a model for how indirect effect can be, how delayed, how invisible; no one is more hopeful than a writer, no one is a bigger gambler'. For most of the years she has spent writing and rewriting sentences, Solnit concedes, 'the difference between throwing something in the trash and publishing it was imperceptible'. But more recently her work has started pinging back to her from all over the world, as it reached a reader in some long-delayed and unexpected way. 'You scatter your seeds,' she writes. 'Rats might eat them, or they might rot. In California, some seeds lie dormant for decades because they only germinate after fire, and sometimes the burned landscape blooms most lavishly.'[25]

No truly worthwhile act has any surety of return. All creative work is a long-odds wager with our time and our lives. Books get pulped and shredded into road aggregate. Plays are performed to half-full auditoria for a fortnight before the theatre goes dark. Films project into cinemas where paying customers fall asleep in the comfy chairs. A TV actor performs her big scene drowned out by the sound of thousands of hairdryers, vacuum cleaners and living-room arguments. 'All work is as seed sown,' wrote Thomas Carlyle. 'Who shall compute what effects have been produced, and are still, and into deep Time, producing?' Many seeds are scattered; most fall on stones. Art is a dead letter with no name on the envelope, sent into the void.

The fruits of creativity are asynchronous and asymmetrical – a suspended dialogue with the absent and the yet to be born. All we can do is keep the faith that our lone acts of creation occur, like the movements of flocking starlings or shoaling fish, in tandem with others, and that they will one day feed into the accumulated beauty and wisdom of the world. Every creative act joins in this eternal symphony of human life. Failure is the price we pay for our place in the orchestra.

6.

The Crooked Timber of Humanity

Or why failure is only human

When I was growing up, adulthood felt like a glorious state of completion. It meant being able very casually to unlock a car, uncork a wine bottle, or pay the bill in a restaurant by miming a scribbled signature at the waiter and fishing a chequebook out of a top pocket without having first to pat one's breast to check it was still there. With what superhuman self-possession did this race of giants manage to trap the receiver under their chins while talking on the phone, or ignite a cigarette lighter on the first flick! I mistook the ordinary proficiency of the late-twentieth-century adult for evidence of glamour and savoir faire. The grown-ups just seemed so effortlessly expert at *life*.

Many children, I have since found, feel the same. Our classic children's books sentimentalize childhood as a charmed land glimpsed longingly from the fallen state of adulthood. Children's films, too, often have a set storyline of a workaholic father who must be taught by a child how to re-enter the enchanted realm. We forget that, unlike Peter Pan or Christopher Robin, most children can't wait to grow up. They long to leave Neverland or the Hundred Acre Wood and arrive at that bewitching but far-removed place, adulthood. Childhood for them is a sentence to be served, a skin to be shed, a state to be overthrown. Just being a grown-up, with no one treating you as a subordinate, feels radical and exciting enough.

As adults, we forget ever feeling like this, and so we also forget that adulthood is a hard-won achievement. The baby boomers of my parents' generation whose maturity I so admired as a child took short, linear paths to adulthood. Many were married with children, pensions and their own homes by their early twenties. They seemed to slide easily into adulthood as if it were as inevitable a life stage as puberty – but perhaps, like most things, it was not as simple as it looked.

Nowadays being grown up is more complicated and *adult* has turned into a verb. *Adulting* to a twenty-something means doing some grown-up task, particularly a mundane one like watering plants, ironing clothes or wiring a plug. The baby boomers had secure work, final salary pensions and cheap mortgages to smooth their journey to adulthood. The young adults who dabble in adulting today have no such path to follow and find themselves stranded in semi-maturity, with grown-up bodies but without a script, wondering how to act their age.

The word *adulting* is meant self-mockingly. It recognizes that adulthood means doing the dull, basic stuff and not expecting applause. But it is also a word used wistfully by those denied many of the perks of adulthood enjoyed by their parents. Forced to do hourly-paid work while still living at home or in rented rooms, they feel, and no wonder, suspended in limbo between adolescence and midlife.

One feature of our austere times has been a pointless sneering at the young by their elders. For having the temerity to want a stable job or an affordable house, they are dismissed as snowflakes and told to grow up and quit whingeing. If only the sneerers knew how much hidden tenacity, low cunning and wheedling charm a young person has to draw on today to get through the boring business of living.

Most of life is admin. Young adults waste hulking portions of their lives looking for places to live, dealing with bad landlords, or applying for and moving between jobs in that cruelly misnamed and emotionally depleting space, the gig economy. All paid work requires skill and stamina. There is no such thing as an unskilled job, as we would soon discover were we asked to prepare and pull a shot on an espresso machine, retrieve change from a till or clean a hotel room as quickly as a chambermaid has to. Often the toughest task in life is negotiating the dreary stuff without screaming or folding ourselves into a weeping ball. 'We are not saints, but we have kept our appointment,' Vladimir says in *Waiting for Godot*. 'How many people can boast as much?' Estragon replies: 'Billions.' Just showing up is hard enough. Every life is its own act of heroism, even if – no, especially if – it ends in failure.

Deep into adulthood I may be, but still what makes me feel most like a failure is my ongoing attempt at adulting. All visible evidence to the contrary, I still imagine myself as the youngest and callowest person in any gathering. Being left-handed, poorly coordinated and unathletic, I move through the world gauchely and dyspraxically. I prod uselessly at my smartphone while the digital virtuosos around me swipe and pinch theirs like musical instruments, to book cabs and hotel rooms and navigate unfamiliar streets. Often my phone disowns me, refusing to recognize my thumbprint and unlock itself.

I came late to the usual motor-skill rites of passage, such as learning to swim or ride a bike. I failed my driving test four times and only passed on my fifth go because the examiner took pity on me when I made a hash of my parallel parking. 'We use our discretion,' he said with a wink after telling me that I had passed. This well-intentioned rule bend meant only that I felt I had failed in spirit, and drove nervously for years afterwards, unsure if I should be on the road.

Then there is my body's knack for failing me at inauspicious moments. My voice has a penchant for cracking up when I am most dependent on it, such as in the middle of lectures. At my first paper at an academic conference, I fainted with sleep deprivation and nerves, and the panel chair had to read out my paper while I sat shamed in a corner of the room, trying not to be sick.

Yet for most of my life I have been able to offer a persuasive impression of a responsible and functioning adult. I got out of bed when the alarm went off, turned up for work on time, made my way to and from the places I needed to be at, knew where to stand and what to say on cue, answered my voicemails and met my deadlines. I am fairly sure that others thought me satisficingly competent, equitable and sane. And still this never felt like real adulting, it being reached through such a cloud of self-lacerating anxiety, even if the cloud could only be seen by me.

One winter's day in 1964, a bitter one even by the standards of the upper Midwest, Raymond Carver sat in a packed laundromat in Iowa City doing several loads of washing. He was twenty-five, married with two young children, and broke. He had come to Iowa from the West Coast to enrol at the university's Writers' Workshop, but it made him homesick and shy. His dream of being a writer seemed more remote than ever.

The laundromat was not usually a depressing place. It was around the corner from Carver's favourite beer joints, and sometimes he chatted there with a writer-couple, Clark Blaise and Bharati Mukherjee, as they struggled to maintain a supply of clean diapers for their baby. That afternoon, though, Carver was on his own and anxiously watching the dryers in use. When one of them became free, he planned to commandeer it for the basket of damp clothes he had been tending for half an hour. He had already missed out twice because someone had beaten him to a dryer, and was panicking because he had to pick his kids up.

At last he saw the tumbling clothes in one dryer slow down, then lie still. The unwritten law of the laundromat was that if no one claimed the sedentary clothes within 30 seconds he could replace them with his. But just as the half-minute was up, a woman came over, opened the dryer, decided her clothes weren't dry enough and fed the dryer more dimes.

At that moment, Carver wrote later, he saw that his life was 'a small-change thing for the most part, chaotic, and without much light showing through'.[1] Up to that point, he had believed that hard work and good intentions would one day be rewarded. Now, trying not to cry at a busy dryer, he could see that these virtues weren't enough and that he would never be the writer he wanted to be. The hardscrabble facts of his life didn't allow it.

Carver did go on to be a successful writer, of course, and one whose years of house flits and low-paid work in sawmills, stockrooms and hospitals made him the writer he was. His characters are broken, as he was, by unrewarding jobs, drink, marital rifts and the fear of destitution. They waitress in 24-hour coffee shops on the edge of town, sell vitamins door to door or stay at home drunk, lying on the sofa, listening to the rain and looking through the closed curtains for the mailman. They often have, as Carver did in that laundromat, some ghastly epiphany in which it dawns on them that they will never escape their failed lives. 'Carver focuses on his characters just when they realize that things will be the same for ever,' Bruce Weber writes, 'a realization that ensures that they will never be the same again.'[2]

The tale of the laundromat appears in an essay, 'Fires', which Carver wrote in 1981, by which time he was considered the leading American short-story writer of his era. But what is odd about this essay is that he refuses to execute the usual narrative switchback, to turn the truck around and say 'but look at me now, a famous author'. Instead he recalls the malign effect on his work of having two demanding children and never enough money. He glosses over all the waitressing jobs his wife took on to give him time to write, and all the time he lost to drink, and the 'second life', as he called it, that began on 2 June 1977 – the day he stopped drinking. In 'Fires', there is no sense of before and after, of some long-but-worth-it wait for redemption. Even now, as a successful writer, he still feels that the words he has written are second best to the ones he didn't write because they needed attention he couldn't spare.

At some point in our lives, I think, we all have the same epiphany as Carver. 'Surely you have to succeed, if you give everything you have,' says Florence Green in Penelope Fitzgerald's novel *The Bookshop* – just as she is about to have her dream of running a successful bookshop in a small seaside town squashed by provincial resentments and subterfuge. Her interlocutor, Milo North, replies: 'I can't see why. Everyone has to give everything they have eventually. They have to die. Dying can't be called a success.'[3] North is an oleaginous chancer, but on this point he is right. A lot of us persist in believing, like Florence, that if we try hard enough we are owed some luck – long after we are buried shoulder-deep in counter-evidence.

The discovery may come later in our lives than Carver's did. But in time we learn to accept that we can't always remake ourselves, that every failed moment does not lead to salvation. Our life's great revelation is that we stay the same damaged person we have always been. We can't just pick ourselves up and turn our lives around. Most of us, like Carver holding back tears in that laundromat, are too busy dealing with the never-ending hassle of living.

This awareness turns you, at whatever age it arrives, into a grown-up. Finally the penny drops: your life is a long, unavertable falling into failure.

Your entry into this world was greeted as an extraordinary event. It led you to believe, as Freud put it, that you were a royal baby. In the first few years of your life, reality began to puncture this dream. You had to face up to your failure to be the centre of everyone else's universe. As a human animal, unlike most animals, you were born prematurely, with your brain, nervous system and limbs all undeveloped. It took you years to master even basic functions. So you relied on others to satisfy your needs and, since your needs were narcissistic and all-encompassing, they often failed to meet them.

The child psychoanalyst D. W. Winnicott believed that failing was part of parenting. He thought that the best kind of mother (his views on parenting being of their time) is just 'good enough'. You are only alive because, when you were a helpless infant, a good-enough mother policed what went into your mouth, when you might otherwise have choked or starved. The good-enough mother satisfies the child's basic needs for food, love and safety. But she fails to meet their every need – because when this happens, the child thinks that the world resolves itself by magic. The perfect mother is a mirage who will be too rudely replaced by cruel reality. The good-enough mother inducts her child into the deficiencies of the world.

In a radio talk on step-parents, Winnicott argued for the value of 'the unsuccess story'. Many mothers feel that they don't love their babies enough, failing to see that 'love is a thing that may come but it cannot be turned on'. Often these mothers are more than good enough, and it is better to be mothered by one who is humanly conflicted than by one 'for whom all is easy and smooth, who knows all the answers, and is a stranger to doubt'.[4] Like Freud, Winnicott believed that every healthy ego concedes the inevitability of failure. A proper grown-up is a depressive realist who accepts that life is knotty and unfair and that our plans will often be foiled. Life's biggest challenges can't be solved, only outgrown.

As a young adult, your ambitions were unbounded by time or space. Your life seemed limitless – stretching out to infinity in front of you, far longer than you had already lived, which already felt like a long time because your first years on earth were a distant dream-memory. Then, very gradually and without you noticing at first, your life began to shrink. It turned out to be shorter than you thought, and always filling up with the tedious work of sustenance, maintenance and recuperation that you forgot to factor in.

You once thought of your body, insofar as you noticed it at all, as the reliable vehicle for getting you where you needed to be. But now, suddenly, you are older. You notice that the body that you took so for granted can't be relied upon after all. You used to think of illness the way you thought of failure – that is, because you secretly feared it, you built narratives of character-forming transcendence around it. The wellness industry convinced you that if you optimized your health and fitness you could master your fate, that ageing could be solved by willpower.

The poet and essayist Anne Boyer, writing about the positivity demanded of women with breast cancer, calls it 'a test designed so everyone will fail', after which 'we all feel like failures, but each of us thinks we have failed alone'. Boyer sees illness as an unavoidable appointment with our 'un-oneness', an encounter with 'pain's leaky democracies, the shared vistas of the terribly felt'.[5]

And yet the language we use to describe bodily decline equates it with personal failure: hearing *loss*, *failing* eyesight, organ *failure*. You *fall* ill, as if you had stumbled on the righteous path to wellbeing. You have medical *examinations*, followed by *tests*, then *test results*. In the consulting room you are back at school again, only this time you need your unbiddable body to get you through the exam. These are tests that we all, in the end, fail. Illness is ordinary, unsurprising, levelling. Your body is just a mass of carbon-based matter, wound up and set working for a few short years until, like an old car with too many miles on the clock, it will refuse to start.

No shame should attach to this kind of failure, for it comes to us all. Everyone alive is exposed and susceptible – walking wounded. You may chase success in the belief that you are immortal; but, by virtue of being alive, you have already failed. Every life, at its end, is a failed experiment – but conducting the experiment is reason enough to live it, because every one of the experiments is different and beautiful in its own way. Being a grown-up means taking responsibility for the experiment of your life, without looking for some actual or imaginary parent to stamp it with their blessing. It means accepting that failure is the small print in the terms and conditions of being human – an occupational hazard of living.

We are born dying, as Heidegger said. One way we protect ourselves from this distressing truth is with something called a *career*. The word *career* originally meant a racecourse or racetrack. Its source was the Latin *carrus*, for 'wheeled vehicle', from which also comes *car*. By extension, *career* came to mean a gallop, a swift course, rapid and continuous progress.

The notion of a career as the course of one's working life, with constant opportunities for advancement, did not fully develop until the early twentieth century. Our identities came to rest heavily on the paid work that we did. Anyone who had not turned their life into a career trajectory was now in danger of being seen as less of a citizen, a partial person – a failure.

In 2010, Melanie Stefan, a neurobiologist at Caltech, proposed an idea in an article in *Nature*. Most of the research fellowships Stefan applied for she did not get – predictably enough, since they were much sought-after and so had low success rates. When she learnt that the Brazilian footballer Ronaldinho had been left out of the 2010 World Cup squad, she felt better about these failures. Ronaldinho had been one of Brazil's stars in the previous two World Cups. Brazil's World Cup squads are announced with some fanfare, so Ronaldinho's failure to make the cut was very public. It made Stefan wonder why failure in sport was so visible and academic failure so hidden. 'As scientists, we construct a narrative of success that renders our setbacks invisible both to ourselves and to others,' she wrote.[6] A scholarly career came to seem like a simple accretion of solid achievement, with no sign of our statistically inevitable friend, failure.

Stefan suggested that scholars compile an alternative CV listing all the things they had failed at. It would be much longer than their normal CV, she warned them, but it would give a truer picture of a scholar's life. Thus inspired, Johannes Haus-hofer, a Princeton psychology professor, released his 'CV of failures'. He arranged it under CV-like subheadings, such as 'degree programs I did not get into', 'paper rejections from academic journals' and 'awards and scholarships I did not get'. Haushofer's CV of failures became a viral hit – garnering more attention, he complained, than anything on his standard CV.

A CV of failures is a sweet and well-meant conceit. But still it relies on the familiar folk tale that treats failure as something that can always be spun into success, as Rumpelstiltskin spins gold from straw. Only tenured, successful scholars tend to produce CVs of failure. They make their failures public to inspire their junior colleagues on short-term contracts to shrug off disappointment and continue their ascent to the professional heights.

A true curriculum vitae, a faithful record of the course of one's life, would include not just the failures but the bits of uncompleted life that never even got to the stage where they could fail. It would include that large part of our lives made up of wasted time, false starts, aimless worrying and fruitless moaning. It would include all the lost hours we spent daydreaming about the life lived by our better self – the one who is quick-witted and silver-tongued where we are docile and tongue-tied, the one who acts with the clarity and integrity of a Hollywood hero where our motivations are mixed up and scattershot, the one who fulfils the dreams that we are too busy daydreaming to fulfil.

A CV sees a life as a patient accrual of qualifications and esteem indicators, building up line by line to make an impressive, appointable whole. But a true CV would recognize our lives as a slow falling away, an education in the gentle art of losing. There would be room on that résumé for all our skills that have atrophied and all the things we have half-forgotten, like that single, semi-right fact about crop rotation we retain from the geography exam we sat thirty years ago.

These days I am required to update my own CV online using – oh, that bane of modern working life, the four-noun string – a *Research Information Management System*. My professional achievements must now be constantly updated and publicly displayed. In the olden days academics could make fine, forgiving distinctions between a piece of writing that was *in press*, *under contract* or just (absolving participle!) *ongoing*. Now the software creates a merciless line graph of our 'research outputs' by year, so it may reveal our fallow periods and prompt us to address any performance shortfall.

This CV I worked so hard to build now seems so measly compared to the ambitions I started out with. Is this dull display of ISBN numbers, dates and page runs really all I have to show for those years of deadline-dogged, fretful work? My CV brings back word from a spectral life, lived out in a neatly tabulated, greyscale world in 12-point Arial font. Under bold subheadings like 'employment history' and 'professional service', I deposited my life, chopped and cubed into bullet points, as if the universe was keeping score. The gaps in my CV faintly embarrass me. But inside those gaps I was just living my life, dealing with the usual crises and griefs, or getting through the day-devouring tedium of adulting.

The curriculum vitae is life as marketing exercise. It sees us as a rigid container of skillsets and credentials. It reduces us to the languages we speak, the IT packages we can competently use and our outside interests in fell walking and shanty singing. It affixes adjectives to ourselves – *proactive, detail-oriented, client-focused* – that we would never dream of using elsewhere. We slot ourselves into the template, but we might as well squeeze a sponge into a cigarette packet. Like Dorian Gray's ageless face, the CV displays an image of perfection in place of the messily mortal self we hide from others and from ourselves. How crushing, then, that even this buffed and glossed version of us is so often met with the formula vapidity of the rejection letter: *Thank you for your interest . . . large number of applications . . . sorry to inform you that on this occasion . . . good luck with your job search . . .*

In his book *The Comedy of Survival*, Joseph Meeker considers two ways that human culture has come to terms with the certainty of failure: tragedy and comedy. In tragedy, the male hero exists in a state of conflict with some force – nature, the gods, death, his own self-defeating desires – that will ultimately overthrow him. He tries to escape his human limits and fails. The audience feels both awe and pity for him as he follows this doomed passion to its end. The tragic hero is ennobled by failure – like Sophocles' Oedipus, who, even as he stabs his eyes out and prepares to go into exile, has learnt to live with this punishment for his carelessness and hubris.

The ancient Greeks liked to imagine themselves as disillusioned dreamers and martyrs to their ideals, just as we do. Tragedy would not exist were self-pity not so pleasurable. When a human being laments that their life is a failure, they speak like a tragic hero. They mean that they have failed within some closed circle of meaning they have made for themselves, stepped inside and mistaken for the world. Our ideas of failure, and the meanings we attach to the word itself, are human inventions. Arguably, failure doesn't even exist in the non-human world; it needs us meaning-making mammals to call it into being.

Chinua Achebe's novel *Things Fall Apart* relates the tragedy of an Igbo leader, Okonkwo, in southern Nigeria in the 1890s. His whole life consists of proving his masculinity, as a way of living down the memory of his gentle, lazy, debt-ridden father. He becomes a wrestling champion and a brave fighter, and fills his barns full of yams – for yams, unlike beans and cassava, are a proper man's crop. But then Okonkwo kills a boy because an oracle tells him to, and because he fears losing face among the men of the village if he does not. Finally, to avoid the shame of being tried by a colonial court, he kills himself – a moral outrage in Igbo teachings. His name is ever after associated with shameful failure.

The lesson of *Things Fall Apart*, and of all tragedy, is that we pin our self-respect to the most dubious masts. Suicidal shame may result from a rotting yam harvest as it does in Achebe's novel, or from an online spat. Tragic heroes assign mystical properties to the respect they earn, or fail to earn, from others. They believe that failure is irredeemable disgrace.

Comedy, for Meeker, sees failure quite differently. It laughs in the face of tragedy's heroic poses and high-flown ideals. It distrusts tragic emotions like passionate love or hate, and all the bloated language of honour that leads, in tragedy, to war and death. Where tragedy demands that fatal choices be made, comedy prefers the botched compromise that allows everyone to go on living. Where tragedy puffs up our species pride, our shared fantasy that the universe gives a fig for our beliefs and longings, comedy bids us respond to our human limitations not with shame but with laughter. It tells us that our naked, animal bodies are ridiculous, but never mind. The comic hero is both clown and sage, the unmasker of pomposity and cant in what Shakespeare's Falstaff calls 'this foolish-compounded clay, man'.

What matters in comedy is not who wins and loses but the game of life itself. The comic way seeks to enjoy and sustain life, because it knows that life is all there is. In Aristophanes' comedy *Lysistrata*, the heroine leads the women of Athens and Sparta on a sex strike to try and end the Peloponnesian War. The play's finale, with a banquet for Athenians and Spartans in the Acropolis where husbands and wives pair up again, reveals no great truth. It only returns us, via the wit and wiliness of the women, to a flawed but liveable normality.

Goscinny and Uderzo's Asterix books all end similarly, with a banquet under a starry sky. This plucky little corner of northern Gaul has held out against the Roman invaders once more – not because Asterix is a superhero (the local druid Getafix's magic potion confers irresistible strength on him for just a few minutes) but because, like a true comedian, he has made the most of his cunning and luck.

Comic heroes rarely succeed but they always survive. In Buster Keaton's famous stunt in *Steamboat Bill, Jr.*, the entire frontage of a house collapses on him during a cyclone, only for him to emerge unscathed through the gap made by an attic window left open. Comic heroes survive not by being heroic but by standing in just the right place at the right time, or by running away. In *Henry IV, Part I*, Falstaff claims to have killed Hotspur when in fact he has feigned death rather than fight. In *City Lights*, Charlie Chaplin simpers and bats his eyelashes at his boxing opponent in the locker room and, when in the ring, hides behind the referee and throws sneaky punches. In *Catch-22*, American Air Force bombardier Yossarian has one mission each time he flies: to come down alive. His ultimate ambition is to be grounded as insane. He fails to achieve it because of that famous 'catch': anyone who wants to get out of combat duty can't be crazy.

The comic hero does not live happily ever after so much as carry on living. At the end of *Some Like It Hot*, Geraldine (Jack Lemmon) tells her sugar daddy Osgood, while taking off her wig, that they can't get married because she's a man. Osgood replies with the film's famous last line and comedy's enduring lesson: 'Well, nobody's perfect.'

The comic hero must come to terms with being trapped in a less-than-perfect life. Charlie Brown will always tree that kite, always lead his baseball team to defeat, always miss the football when Lucy swipes it away, always search his mailbox for missing valentines from the little red-haired girl – and always learn to bear those failures and stay hopeful and tender-hearted.

Tony Hancock, Harold Steptoe, Captain Mainwaring, Basil Fawlty, David Brent. The classic British sitcom characters are all inveterate failures, entombed in unhappy situations by their own male self-regard. The same goes for Del Boy Trotter in *Only Fools and Horses*, who drives a three-wheeled van with 'New York – Paris – Peckham' painted on its side and is convinced that 'this time next year we'll be millionaires'. But then the Trotters actually *do* become millionaires, by discovering a John Harrison watch in their lock-up garage, at which point you know the sitcom has lost its way. Comic heroes must never be successful. We laugh at their failures on the condition that nothing too tragic will befall them either, that they will at least be allowed to go on with their disappointing lives. They may be venal and ridiculous, may lose their dignity and even their trousers – but they endure.

Comedy mocks our delusions of grandeur, the whole sorry business of power play and status-seeking. Almost as old as medal-making is the comic counter-tradition of the mocking medal. Louis XIV's enemies commissioned medals of the Sun King falling from his chariot or romping with his mistress. One 1689 medal by a Dutch artist has Louis vomiting money into a chamber pot while the Pope gives him an enema. In 1713, the German medal-maker Christian Wermuth fashioned a medal of the signatories of the Treaty of Utrecht – Britain, France and Holland – as a council of defecating arseholes. The medal's reverse shows the three countries a year later, throwing their shit at each other.

In 1933, the caricaturist George de Zayaz designed a medal shaped like a lavatory seat in 'honour' of the American senator Huey Long. It commemorated the punch that Long received for drunkenly peeing on another man's leg at a urinal. In 1967, Marcel Duchamp editioned a medal in silver, bronze and steel entitled *Bouche-évier (Sink Stopper)*, a cast of a plug he had made for the shower of his Catalonian holiday home because he wanted to wash his feet. With this medal, shaped from the plughole that drained his own human muck, Duchamp outed himself as a comedian.

Medals are meant to lift us sublimely out of our own dirt and waste. Mocking medals do the opposite, by showing that we are stuck in our unreliable – shitting, pissing, puking, sweating – bodies. They are *memento culpa*, reminders of our defective selves. Success is a short-lived game, they say, and failure our natural state.

At the time of writing, the United States has a president who sees himself as a tragic hero. According to his swollen rhetoric of boast and insult, people are only ever winners or losers. Success must be bought, in a desolate game of competitive maleness, at the expense of someone else's failure. He assaults his enemies with steamrollering words like *sad*, *dumb* and *failing*. A favourite term of opprobrium is *loser* – a word he has applied (preceded by intensifiers like *stone-cold* and *total*) to Cher, Russell Brand, Alan Sugar, teachers, terrorists, CNN presenters and the Huffington Post, among others.

In response, the president's enemies point out that he is not a tragic hero at all but a bawling man-child. They mock his fake tan, sell toilet paper bearing an image of his face, likewise toilet brushes with orange bristles that mimic his unruly head of hair, or fly him as a blubbing baby blimp in a nappy. They cut through his Shakespearean bad-boy bluster to reveal the bruised ego and mortal shell beneath. Much to his annoyance, and despite his having no discernible sense of humour, they have turned him into a comedian.

Tragedy, Meeker writes, is an invention of western civilization, specifically of the Athenians in the fifth century BCE and of cultures inspired by them, such as Elizabethan and Jacobean London. But comedy exists everywhere, even in nature. It grows artlessly out of life's biological realities. Plants and animals live the comic way in their pragmatism and pliability. Evolution is a sort of comedy, its aim being to allow life to thrive in all its myriad forms. The living things that thrive are not those best able to destroy the competition – a common misreading of Darwin's phrase 'the survival of the fittest' – but those that can stay alive. Healthy ecosystems maintain an equilibrium that avoids all-or-nothing rivalries and fosters diversity. In an ecosystem, what matters is not individual success or failure but maintaining the delicate organic whole.

Evolution has no interest in the ideal solution; it simply eliminates the unworkable and settles for the good enough. A crocodile looks nearly identical to its fossil ancestors that lived eighty million years ago. The crocodile's genes found a workaround, a good-enough way of existing, and stuck with it. In evolution, anything that doesn't kill you is fine. As in comedy, success in nature means finding a way to survive.

Sometimes living things flourish, taking on lushness and weight; sometimes they pare right back. A deciduous tree sheds its greenery in autumn so it can conserve energy and water and attend to its roots. What looks like a beautiful death is all about preserving life. Plants survive the winter as dormant seeds, tubers and bulbs. Animals bed down, slow their metabolic rates and live off their store of seeds or humps of fat. Nature's gift is for survival. With our human talent for dissatisfaction, we forget what an accomplishment that is.

Here is one compensation of getting older: it turns us into comedians by default. 'In middle age a liberation takes place,' the poet Michael Hamburger once wrote. A fourth element appears alongside the id, ego and superego, 'smiling or unashamedly laughing at their silly little squabbles'. This fourth element is a relativist not an absolutist, a comedian not a tragedian. The middle-aged are converts to life's essential absurdity. Diana Athill writes beautifully about old age as 'like coming out onto a high plateau, into clear, fresh air, far above the antlike bustle going on down below me'. [7] I hope one day to feel like this too. I will be an unembittered onlooker, with only benign feelings towards those still stuck in the land stretching out below me, where success matters more than survival and failure is a kind of death. If anyone knows a way to attain this elevated state, please tell me how.

In 1973, the American author Seymour Krim published a sad, scab-picking essay, 'For my Brothers and Sisters in the Failure Business'. He wrote it after a sometime friend, sore because Krim had given his book a bad review, sent him a telegram calling him a failure, someone who 'spent his snivelling days carving up his betters'. Krim, living in Paris at the time, felt 'the dirty American word "failure" wing its way across the water and hit me where it hurts'.

Krim was hardly a failure. He wrote for the big newspapers and magazines, published a few books that got noticed, won Guggenheim and Fulbright fellowships, and taught creative writing at Columbia and Iowa. But he thought himself a nearly man, hawking his talents in that unwieldy, unmarketable form that publishers and booksellers hate: the essay. At school, he had been a pimply-faced nerd. He saw writing as a competitive sport, a way to take revenge on the school peers who had thought him uncool. He wrote candidly about being eaten alive by a need to be swooned over at all the right parties and his envy of more successful authors – a long list that included three of his contemporaries at DeWitt Clinton High School in the Bronx: James Baldwin, Paddy Chayefsky (the Oscar-winning screenwriter) and Stan Lee (creator of Spider-Man, the Fantastic Four and the X-Men). By his own measure, and that of the rivalrous New York scene he inhabited, he had failed.

By the time he wrote 'For my Brothers and Sisters in the Failure Business', Krim was fifty-one. He had spent years checking in and out of mental hospitals and failing to finish his big novel.

This essay was the last major piece he published. He wasted most of the next decade writing a dense, thousand-page, paragraph-free, unpublished prose-poem about American life called *Chaos*. In 1989, crippled by heart disease, he overdosed on barbiturates in his one-room, cold-water apartment on East 10th Street, New York.

For all this grim backdrop, 'For my Brothers and Sisters' is not a grim read. If Krim's fuel in his early work was fame-thirsty desperation, his tone here is more resigned. The essay is a stoic and comradely note to other failures, full of self-pity but flecked with self-awareness. Instead of just writing about himself and his tribe of overachieving Manhattanites as usual, he reaches out to other failures, those 'always living on the lip of hope'.

Our secret, Krim explains to his siblings in failure, is that we cling to an exalted vision of some better version of ourselves, even 'as we fumble with the unglamorous pennies of life during the illusionless middle years'. It is a fine and unshaming thing to have tried and failed, he declares, even if failure does feel worse as you get older – and those who once saw you 'robed in the glow of your vision' now see only 'an unmade bed and a few unwashed cups on the bare wooden table of a gray day'.[8]

How could one not be won over by that unforgettable, big-hearted title? 'Brothers and Sisters in the Failure Business' is just right. We can't choose our siblings like we can our friends. But we are linked to them by shared histories and tacit sympathies that even the closest friends don't have. Brothers and sisters know things about each other that the rest of the world never will. We don't even have to like each other to draw on such unabashed intimacy. We are brothers and sisters in failure, whether we like it or not.

Being human means being a failure. It means committing ourselves to plans that we know will break down or peter out into nothingness. It means making the most of our one, finite, corporeal life even when this seems like a fool's errand, a gamble with impossible odds and never enough time.

In her essay 'Transcending Humanity', the philosopher Martha Nussbaum wonders why the gods and goddesses of Greek myth keep falling in love with us mortals. Why is the beautiful, ageless Calypso so smitten with Odysseus? Shouldn't she prefer the eternal perfection of her own kind? Nussbaum decides that, like other immortals, Calypso is drawn to the ferocity and brightness with which we mortals burn – to our verve, ingenuity and stubborn snatching at happiness in the face of our short lives and certain deaths. That gated community of gods on Mount Olympus, who move us around their cosmic chessboard like expendable pawns, love us for not being pampered, callous and jaded like them – because, unlike them, we fail.[9]

In Homer's epics, each beating human heart sustains a micro-bead of ego, full of fear and hope, which is snuffed out at a stroke as we 'go down to death'. To the Greeks, life was all the more precious for being so precarious, so bound up in our fleshy and fragile bodies. That is why Odysseus chooses his own, time-limited life with Penelope over a deathless life with Calypso. To a human being, a god's life seems lifeless, even inconceivable. Only a life with failure and loss in it feels worth living. We are most fully human when we care deeply about someone or something that will die or be lost, when we love the world and its other occupants even though we know that our own time is short and our best efforts come to naught.

Our mortality fills our lives with confusion and pain and ends them in failure, but it also makes every life treasurable. The Talmud asks: why did God create only one Adam? First, it says, He wanted to prevent men from feeling superior to one another by giving them the same ancestor. Second, He wanted to show them that any human being is an entire world. God, it says, 'coins all people from Adam's die and not one looks like another'. All of us matter equally because the world would be incomplete without any one of us. The Talmud says that if you kill one person you are as guilty as if you had killed everyone in the world, and if you save one human life you are as heroic as if you had saved every life.

Set alongside the size and age of the universe, or even the history of humanity, a single human life hardly matters at all. But this hard logic isn't how most of us respond to the unsolvable conundrum of being alive. Nor is it how we feel when someone we love dies – because that someone has left a human-shaped hole moulded to their exact dimensions, that can't be filled by anyone or anything else.

When we say that someone is 'only human', we are not just excusing their faults. We are saying that we actually prefer their chaotic non-computability to the soulless perfection of a machine – and that their inimitable failings are precisely what gives their lives incalculable worth. Yiddish has a word, *mensch*, from the German for man. Figuratively it means someone who is honest, honourable, generous and kind – someone doing their best to live a good life. But literally it means 'human being'. For a Jew it is the highest form of praise.

To call any life a failure, or a success, is to miss the infinite granularity, the inexhaustible miscellaneity, of all lives. Every life is incommensurable with any other life. Someone else's success does not make you more of a failure, because their life can never subsume or cancel out yours. Each life runs along its own tracks to its own destination. It can't be compared to anything outside itself, nor judged by any yardstick other than its own. A life can't really succeed or fail at all; it can only be lived.

On 2 May 1519, a failed artist lay dying at Clos Lucé, the manor house next to the Château d'Amboise, the royal residence of his friend King Francis I, in the Loire Valley. On his deathbed, according to his biographer Giorgio Vasari, he repented to the

King that 'he had offended God and mankind in not having worked at his art as he should have done'.

One of many unfinished paintings in his studio was of Lisa Gherardini, the wife of a Florentine silk merchant. He had begun it in 1503, when its subject was a young woman of twenty-four. Now she was nearly forty, and he had neither delivered the painting nor been paid for it. Instead he had taken it with him, unfinished, from Florence to Milan, then Rome, then France, adding little strokes of paint and layers of glaze as he went.

He was a serial dabbler with a deserved reputation for missing deadlines. When Pope Leo X saw him making the varnish for a picture before he had started painting it, he said, 'Alas, this man will never do anything, for he begins to think of the end before the beginning.' His inability to finish lost him many commissions. In his notebooks, full of hundreds of shelved or abandoned schemes, he had scribbled over and over: 'Tell me if anything was ever done.'

Perhaps, on his deathbed, he found himself mourning these failed projects. But which of the many to mourn? Did he grieve for the untold days wasted, over seventeen years, modelling a bronze statue of a rearing horse ridden by Francesco Sforza, the soldier who founded Milan? All that time he had spent studying the movement and musculature of a horse's anatomy was made useless in an instant – when the French conquered Milan and their archers used his clay model for target practice.

Or did he weep for his greatest commission, a fresco of Christ's last supper, painted on a dining-room wall in a Milan monastery? Fresco painting normally required that the paint be applied on to wet plaster. Instead he had caked it on dry plaster using his own experimental mix of water- and oil-based pigments, so that he could keep retouching it. Now, as he lay dying, he knew indisputably that the experiment had failed. After only twenty years, the paint had begun to flake. In a few decades the whole fresco would be made up of blots.

Or did he bewail the hours he had squandered on making jeux d'esprit for the Florentine and Milanese courts? Hollow birds made of wax that flew when they were blown up with air. An inflated bladder that filled an entire room. An automaton shaped like a lion that showered lilies from its chest. The crowds who had gasped at these delights had soon forgotten them, just as they soon forgot the sweet sounds he made on his lira da braccio, the fat fiddle on which he improvised like a blues singer. Music, as he complained in his notebooks, is a brief, unrecordable beauty. (Nowhere in those notebooks does he conceive a prototype gramophone.) 'We do not lack devices for measuring these miserable days of ours,' he wrote, 'in which it should be our pleasure that they be not frittered away without leaving behind any memory of ourselves in the mind of men.'

And why, as his powers waned, had he not at least finished that wretched painting of the Florentine merchant's wife? He was just too tired after spending his nights with cadavers. He had intended his findings on the human anatomy to be published but failed to get round to it – probably because he was also busy failing to solve a problem posed by Euclid to do with right-angled triangles. The very last line of his notebooks explained why he was breaking off from this task. *Perché la minestra si fredda*, it said. *Because the soup is getting cold.*

I won't insult you; you know who this man was. You may even have heard of his failures, now that he has become a poster boy for the failing well movement and those failures are seen as crucial stages on his climb to the Olympian summit of human achievement.

But that is cruel optimism, fake solace. It implies that all us other failures have to do is be more like him. In fact, his rare successes were threaded sparely through a lifetime of solid, reliable failure. They were brief blips in a tale of mostly unswerving disappointment. He neither learnt from his failures nor wished to learn. They were not a series of questions to which his genius was the jubilant answer. They were part of the whole grain of that genius – in the original sense of the word, to mean the unique spirit that a person carries with them through life.

In the days and months after his death, no one mourned those failed schemes and uncompleted masterpieces. They mourned the man himself. For he was, it seems, an exasperatingly scatty but insurmountably lovable friend, far more lovable than his great rival, that tireless networker and CV-builder Michelangelo. His pupil Francesco Melzi witnessed his last hours and wrote shortly afterwards: 'Until the day when my body is laid under the ground, I shall experience perpetual sorrow. His loss is a grief to everyone, for it is not in the power of nature to reproduce another such man.'

No, his life teaches us nothing about the galvanizing or purgative effects of failure. But perhaps it teaches us something else: that failure is human. We are equivocating, time-wasting, self-deceiving, self-sabotaging animals. If the world doesn't screw us up, we will gladly take up the slack and screw things up all by ourselves. Just as a footballer can miss an open goal when it looked easier to score, so we can fail when it would have been much less bother for us just to succeed. There is more than one version of us, and those different versions can make things hard for each other. We fail because we conspire against ourselves.

So what could be more human than a prodigiously gifted artist devising impossible schemes that he kept abandoning for even more impossible schemes? To us fellow procrastinators, his notebooks are reassuringly full of to-do lists of things that never get done. *Ask Benedetto Protinari by what means they walk on ice in Flanders. Inflate the lungs of a pig and observe whether they increase in width and in length, or only in width. Describe the tongue of the woodpecker.* He filled one of his notebooks with his attempts to solve the ancient mathematical puzzle of 'squaring the circle' – which cannot be done with just a compass and ruler, which was all he had. He wasted thousands of hours trying to devise a self-propelled human flying machine, parsing all the permutations – pistons, pedals, gears, pulleys – that might overcome the weakness of our breast muscles. If only he had known that, although the dream is as old as Icarus, no human can fly just by flapping wings.

Other of his schemes were not just theoretical failures but concrete disasters. In 1504, he had hatched a plan with his friend Niccolò Machiavelli to divert the River Arno, so as to cut Pisa off from the sea and allow Milan to reconquer the city without bloodshed. The walls of the diversion ditch ended up collapsing and flooding the nearby farms. The farmers' reactions are unrecorded, but safe to say they were not hailing Leonardo da Vinci as a genius.

Leonardo's whole life was, like one of his paintings, the work of all-too-human hands. A painting, like a life, can't be wholly planned. You can do a few preliminary sketches, camouflage your mistakes as you go along and, in extremis, paint over the whole canvas and start again. But it has to be made in the moment, with the human energy of its brushstrokes. One way that an art expert spots a forgery is that it looks too controlled, too impeccable. The genuine article is always cross-grained, finely woven, fascinatingly fault-ridden – just like the human being who made it. As Leonardo the non-completer knew, every great painting totters on the edge of failure. A single extra dab of paint might enrich it or spoil it – which is why the *Mona Lisa* was only truly finished when its maker's life was over.

The closer you get to a painting, the more the work of human hands it seems. You spot the stray drips of paint, the three-dimensional blobs of impasto, even the loops and whorls of the artist's fingerprints. When you look at a reproduction of Jan Vermeer's *The Milkmaid*, its composition seems impossibly pure – a godlike facsimile of the real, even if one dictated from the Almighty with the aid of a camera obscura. But look at the actual painting in Amsterdam's Rijksmuseum and everything is different. You see that Vermeer applied the paint sculpturally and unevenly, to suggest how light from the window falls on the rough wall plaster, the Delft tiles, the coarsely textured bread crusts and the folds of the white linen cap and blue apron worn by the woman pouring milk so watchfully into a bowl. The most perfect painting looks, up close, humanly made.

Most of the hands stencilled in prehistoric cave art are left hands – because most of those prehistoric artists were right-handers, and so they held the spraying pipe full of ochre dye in their defter hand and traced the weaker one. Great art is made not by demigods but by human beings working within human limits. 'Out of the crooked timber of humanity,' wrote Kant, 'no straight thing was ever made.'

Art is not in the perfection business. 'There is no progress in art, any more than there is progress in making love,' Man Ray wrote. 'There are simply different ways of doing it.' Any work of art is just adding its bit to that intricate human conversation, begun tens of thousands of years ago when Homo sapiens went deep into caves to blow dye on the walls. Art always fails; some of it just fails so exquisitely as to make any prefab vision of success seem beggarly by comparison.

In a human life, as in a painting, only something that can fail can be truly beautiful. In Japan they have a word for this notion: *wabi-sabi*. *Wabi-sabi* accepts that nothing is ever faultless, complete or lasting. Beauty, it contends, has little to do with perfect symmetry or golden means. Unevenness, deficiency and decay give objects, and people, the depth and intensity of real beauty.

In the Japanese art of fixing broken pottery, *kintsugi*, the artist does not disguise the breakage but instead makes it part of the life of the object. They put the broken pieces back together as visibly as possible, using lacquer dusted with powdered gold. Every repaired object is unique, because of the randomness with which each pot shatters and thus the asymmetry of the lines traced in gold. (*Kintsugi* means 'golden joinery'.) We love things, and people, most of all when they seem slightly wonky and weathered. Their loveliness feels unrefined, patinated, born of frailty and fallibility.

Whenever I feel most like a failure, I try to remember this. My life has been like a painting gone wrong. I attempt to fix it by tweaking and tinkering at the edges ad nauseum, until I decide that the whole thing is misconceived and I need to paint over it and start from scratch. Now the canvas is showing its age. The paint has begun to crack, flake and discolour and assume a coating of grime and dust.

The painting that is my life will never be finished, just as I will never feel like an adult. But it remains, in the sense that every life is, a work of art. Not an immaculate masterpiece, should such a thing exist. Not a work that will trouble the great auction houses or hang in the Louvre or the Rijksmuseum. Just something I extemporized in the shambolic course of living it, and that only I could have made with my own hands – out of the crooked timber of humanity. I think I will carry on working on it.

7.

The Republic of Failure

Or why failure feels like coming home

In his poem 'Shame', Richard Wilbur imagines this most dis-agreeable of emotions as a small, crowded nation state. The state of Shame has no foreign policy, other than to avoid offending anyone. No visitor can ever decipher its language, because every citizen's words trail off timidly. The chief domestic product is sheep. The census records the population as zero: no one declares their existence because no one thinks they count. Every one of Shame's inhabitants secretly hopes that the country will be overrun by an army of drunk, naked, laughing and stupidly happy people who will release them from their shame.

If failure were a country too, what would it look like? When I conjure it in my head, I see it as resembling a small, ailing Eastern bloc state towards the end of the Cold War. Here, in the Democratic Republic of Failure, every citizen wears the same stout jacket, the same ill-fitting, acid-wash jeans, the same heavy shoes and cheap haircut. Life goes on in jerry-built tower blocks and decaying tenements, often without hot water or inside toilets. The shelves in the shops are almost empty and there is endless queueing for basic goods. Failure hangs dully in the air. Its smell is a mingled by-product of brown coal, cheap cigarettes and dust from the broken roads – the smell of sadness, lethargy and unspoken shame.

Life in the Republic of Failure is not unbearable, but every aspect of it makes people think there is a better life elsewhere. Everyone looks over with envy at the State of Success – its neighbour to the west beyond the Iron Curtain, with its chic boutiques, cornucopian food halls and houses stuffed with microwaves, dishwashers and colour TVs. But then the wall between the two countries finally comes down, and they get to have these things. Their lives do not suddenly fill up with warmth, light and meaning. Instead they begin to feel a vague but unmistakable *ostalgie*, the word they have invented to describe their nostalgia for the country to the east they have left behind.

Failure once seemed to its citizens like the backward state – always trying, and failing, to catch up with the shining modernity of neighbouring Success. Now they see that Failure was not the underdeveloped sibling of Success but a different state altogether. It dawns on them that their former life, born of poverty and constraint, was at least one where things were shared – where everyone drank the same brand of cheap white wine, used the same scratchy toilet paper and drove the same yellow car with its two-stroke, lawnmower engine. Seen through the soft filter of *ostalgie*, these things now speak to their common humanity. For all its horrors, Failure was a republic: everyone failed together.

If failure is a place, then it is somewhere like this – that we are slightly ashamed to have come from but that tells us something edifying about ourselves. Failure, in Ursula K. Le Guin's words, is 'the place that our rationalizing culture of success denies, calling it a place of exile, uninhabitable, foreign'. We need to enter that dark place to live life in all its fullness and fecundity.

Failure speaks to us of our vulnerability, our precarity, our mortality. It is where we meet and break bread with other weak and wavering mortals. It reminds us, Le Guin writes, that our roots are 'not in the light that blinds, but in the dark that nourishes, where human beings grow human souls'.[1] Failure is not a holding station we pass through on the way to somewhere else. It is its own country, where we must all learn to live.

Whatever our passports say, we are citizens of that Republic of Failure. We can return there whenever we like, and the border guards will never shine a torch in our faces, frisk us or ask the purpose of our visit. No papers are required, no citizenship test must be sat, no oath need be sworn. The self-contentedly successful may spend many years away, and we may envy them their charmed lives from afar – but soon enough they will turn up at the border, ask for admission and be waved through. For it turns out that, behind the swank and swagger, they were just like us. Welcome to Failure, the guards will say, where everyone is allowed to fail and no one need learn from the experience or listen to glib prescriptions about how to turn it into redeeming success.

Failure, in other words, is home. Home can feel too familiar, sometimes claustrophobically so. Staying at or returning home means standing still, and in our culture of restless change that can look like failure. Home can remind you too much of yourself. You might long to escape it all your life, which is fine. But sooner or later you will have to live there, just as you will have to live with yourself. And then, when you feel truly at home, you can fail and fail again – and no one will ever stop loving you for the gorgeous failure that you are.

Notes

So as not to clog up this short book with endnotes, I have only refer-
enced quotations that I thought the reader would find it hard to locate
otherwise. Where possible, I have preferred to give a clue in the text
about where to find it (such as by dating quotes from letters and diaries). Every referencing system, I have come to see, is a failure, falling
somewhere between the two stools of airless completism and slap-
dashery. I promise to fail better next time.

As well as the sources cited in the numbered notes below, the
quotes in chapter 2 from Natalia Ginzburg's essays ('Fantasy Life',
'Laziness', 'My Psychoanalysis' and 'Clueless Travellers') come from
the ebook of *A Place to Live: Selected Essays of Natalia Ginzburg*, translated and edited by Lynne Sharon Schwartz (New York: Seven Stories
Press, 2003). The biographical information about Ginzburg not found
in her own work mostly derives from a book of radio interviews with
her, *It's Hard to Talk About Yourself*, edited by Cesare Garboli and Liza
Ginzburg (Chicago: University of Chicago Press, 2003).

The sections in chapter 3 on the Chinese imperial examination system
draw on Ichisada Miyazaki's *China's Examination Hell: The Civil Service
Examinations of Imperial China* (New Haven, CT: Yale University Press,
1981), Benjamin A. Elman's *A Cultural History of Civil Examinations in Late
Imperial China* (Berkeley, CA: University of California Press, 2000) and
his *Civil Examinations and Meritocracy in Late Imperial China* (Cambridge,
MA: Harvard University Press, 2013). The quotes from Wu Ching-tzu's
The Scholars are taken from Gladys Yang's translation, published in ebook
by Olympia Press (2016). The quotes from Pu Songling's work come from
the ebook of *Strange Tales from a Chinese Studio*, translated and edited by
John Minford (London: Penguin, 2006), apart from 'The Seven Likenesses of a Candidate', which is reprinted whole in Miyazaki, pp. 57–8.

The discussion of Johan Cruyff and Dutch football in chapter 4 relies partly on David Winner's *Brilliant Orange: The Neurotic Genius of Dutch Football* (London: Bloomsbury, 2nd edn, 2010). The translation from Pindar is my own.

I was inspired to write about musical flops (chapter 5) after hearing Adam Gopnik's account of his own experiences touring a musical in a BBC Radio 4 *Point of View* on 6 August 2017; see 'On Musical Theatre' in his *In Mid-Air: Points of View from Over a Decade* (London: Riverrun, 2018). Along with sources cited in the endnotes, the story of Lionel Bart and *Twang!!* in chapter 5 draws on David Roper's *Bart! The Unauthorized Life & Times, Ins and Outs, Ups and Downs of Lionel Bart* (London: Pavilion, 1994) and Peter Rankin's *Joan Littlewood: Dreams and Realities: The Official Biography* (London: Oberon Books, 2014). I made use of the chapter on Paul Potts in Stephen Fothergill's *The Last Lamplighter: A Soho Education* (London: London Magazine Editions, 2000). For Joe Gould's story, I relied on Thomas Kunkel's *Man in Profile: Joseph Mitchell of the New Yorker* (New York: Random House, 2015) and Jill Lepore's *Joe Gould's Teeth* (New York: Vintage, 2017).

The discussion of comedy in chapter 6 draws on Joseph W. Meeker's *The Comedy of Survival: Studies in Literary Ecology* (New York: Scribner's, 1974) and Matthew Bevis's *Comedy: A Very Short Introduction* (Oxford: Oxford University Press, 2013). The information on mocking medals comes mostly from Philip Attwood and Felicity Powell's *Medals of Dishonour* (London: British Museum Press, 2009). The section on Leonardo da Vinci makes use of Walter Isaacson's *Leonardo da Vinci: The Biography* (New York: Simon & Schuster, 2017).

1. Despair Young and Never Look Back

1 Adam Phillips, *Missing Out: In Praise of the Unlived Life* (London: Penguin, 2013), p. xii.
2 James Knowlson, *Damned to Fame: The Life of Samuel Beckett* (London: Bloomsbury, 1996), p. 142.

3 'Aidan Higgins on Beckett in the 1950s' in *Beckett Remembering, Remembering Beckett: Uncollected Interviews with Samuel Beckett and Memories of Those Who Knew Him*, ed. James Knowlson and Elizabeth Knowlson (London: Bloomsbury, 2006), p. 139.

4 Christopher Devenney, 'What Remains?' in *Samuel Beckett's Waiting for Godot: New Edition*, ed. Harold Bloom (New York: Infobase, 2008), p. 118; Knowlson, *Damned to Fame*, p. 420.

5 Samuel Beckett, *Worstward Ho* (London: John Calder, 1983), p. 13.

6 Philip Howard, 'Their great expectations', *The Times*, 31 December 1983.

2. Not Enough, Not Enough

1 Sally Rooney, 'Even if you beat me', *The Dublin Review* 58 (Spring 2015), p. 17.

2 Marianne Weber, *Max Weber: A Biography*, trans. and ed. Harry Zohn (New York: John Wiley & Sons, 1975), pp. 242–3, 264.

3 Scott A. Sandage, *Born Losers: A History of Failure in America* (Cambridge, MA: Harvard University Press, 2005), pp. 11, 131–3, 259, 254.

4 Zenn Kaufman, *How to Run Better Sales Contests* (New York: Harper, 2nd edn, 1948), p. 128.

5 Arthur Miller, *Timebends: A Life* (New York: Harper & Row, 1988), p. 184.

6 Sandage, *Born Losers*, p. 5.

7 Annie Ernaux, *The Years*, trans. Alison L. Strayer (London: Fitzcarraldo Editions, 2017), ebook.

8 Natalia Ginzburg, *Never Must You Ask Me*, trans. Isabel Quigly (London: Michael Joseph, 1973), pp. 164, 62, 105.

9 William Weaver, 'War in a classical voice', *New York Times Book Review*, 5 May 1985; unnamed Italian critic cited in Mary Gordon, 'Surviving history', *New York Times Book Review*, 25 March 1990.

10 Natalia Ginzburg, *Family Lexicon*, trans. Jenny McPhee (London: Daunt Books, 2018), ebook.

11 Ginzburg, *Never Must You Ask Me*, pp. 42–3.

12 Ian Thomson, 'Family and friends: A conversation in Rome with Natalia Ginzburg', *London Magazine*, 1 August 1985, p. 61.

13 P. R. Clance and S. A. Imes, 'The imposter phenomenon in high achieving women: Dynamics and therapeutic intervention', *Psychotherapy: Theory, Research & Practice* 15, 3 (Fall 1978), pp. 241–7.

14 Michelle Obama, *Becoming* (London: Viking, 2018), p. 56.

15 Ginzburg, *Never Must You Ask Me*, p. 105.

16 Natalia Ginzburg, *The Little Virtues*, trans. Dick Davis (London: Daunt Books, 2018), pp. 153, 167.

17 Ginzburg, *The Little Virtues*, pp. 105, 107–8.

3. The Examination Dream

1 Sigmund Freud, *The Interpretation of Dreams* (Pelican Freud Library Volume 4), trans. James Strachey, ed. Angela Richards (Harmondsworth: Penguin, 1976), pp. 377–8.

2 Michael Young, *The Rise of the Meritocracy 1870–2033: An Essay on Education and Equality* (Harmondsworth: Penguin, 1961), p. 41.

3 R. H. Tawney, *Equality* (London: Unwin Books, 1964), p. 106.

4 Young, *Rise of the Meritocracy*, p. 103.

5 Young, *Rise of the Meritocracy*, p. 59.

6 Alan Bennett, 'The History Boys' in *Untold Stories* (London: Faber & Faber/Profile, 2005), pp. 394, 396.

7 Alan Barr, 'Pu Songling and the Qing examination system', *Late Imperial China* 7, 1 (June 1986), pp. 102–3.

8 Barr, 'Pu Songling', p. 90.

9 Tawney, *Equality*, p. 105.

4. Life Is Hell, But at Least There Are Prizes

1 Mark Doty, *Firebird: A Memoir* (London: Vintage, 2001), p. 2.

2 Janet Frame, 'Prizes' in *The Daylight and the Dust: Selected Short Stories* (London: Virago, 2010), pp. 115, 122.

3 Virginia Woolf, *Three Guineas* (London: Hogarth Press, 1991), p. 108.

4 Woolf, *Three Guineas*, p. 100.

5 Cynthia Haven, *Evolution of Desire: A Life of René Girard* (East Lansing, MI: Michigan State University Press, 2018), p. 91.

6 See René Girard, *Deceit, Desire and the Novel: Self and Other in Literary Structure* (Baltimore, MD: Johns Hopkins University Press, 1966).

7 Donald Hall, 'A Yeti in the District' in *Essays After Eighty* (Boston: Mariner Books, 2015), p. 26.

8 Haven, *Evolution of Desire*, p. 89.

9 Judith Halberstam, *The Queer Art of Failure* (Durham, NC: Duke University Press, 2011), p. 93.

10 Edward de Bono, *Lateral Thinking: Creativity Step by Step* (New York: Harper Perennial, 1990), pp. 183–5.

11 Eduardo Galeano, *Football in Sun and Shadow*, trans. Mark Fried (London: Penguin, 2018), ebook.

12 Galeano, *Football in Sun and Shadow*.

13 Kevin Keegan, *My Life in Football: The Autobiography* (London: Pan, 2019), p. 99.

14 Roger Kahn, *The Boys of Summer* (London: Aurum Press, 2013), pp. 89, 92, xx, xii.

15 Virginia Woolf, 'Am I a Snob?' in *Moments of Being: Unpublished Autobiographical Writings* (London: Hogarth Press, 1978), p. 185.

5. None of Us Is Proust

1 Len Deighton, *Len Deighton's London Dossier* (London: Jonathan Cape, 1967), p. 203.

2 David Wright, 'Instead of a poet', *Poetry Quarterly*, Winter 1950–51, pp. 247–8; Paul Potts, *Instead of a Sonnet (The 1944 Edition with Ten New Poems)* (London: Tuba Press, 1978), p. 4.

3 Laurie Lee, 'Chelsea Bun' in *Village Christmas: And Other Notes on the English Year* (London: Penguin, 2015), ebook.

4 Dustjacket copy of Paul Potts, *Invitation to a Sacrament* (London: Martin Brian & O'Keeffe, 1973); Alan Ross, 'Not taking it easy', *Times Literary Supplement*, 27 May 1960, p. 341; Stephen Spender, 'The problem of sincerity', *Listener*, 26 May 1960, p. 945.

5 Paul Potts, 'As I went walking down the Charing Cross Road', *Listener*, 26 April 1962, pp. 731, 735.

6 Marc Napolitano, *Oliver! A Dickensian Musical* (Oxford: Oxford University Press, 2014), p. 105.

7 Jean Baudrillard, *Cool Memories*, trans. Chris Turner (London: Verso, 1990), pp. 222–3.

8 John Osborne, *Almost a Gentleman: An Autobiography Vol II: 1955–1966* (London: Faber & Faber, 1991), p. 128; Noël Coward, *The Noël Coward Diaries*, ed. Graham Payn and Sheridan Morley (London: Phoenix Press, 2000), p. 409.

9 Osborne, *Almost a Gentleman*, pp. 126–7.

10 Paul Potts, *Dante Called You Beatrice* (London: Eyre & Spottiswoode, 1960), pp. 105, 154, 34, 57, 17, 35.

11 Adrian Wright, *Must Close Saturday: The Decline and Fall of the British Musical Flop* (Woodbridge: The Boydell Press, 2017), p. 48.

12 Adrian Wright, *A Tanner's Worth of Tune: Rediscovering the Post-war British Musical* (Woodbridge: The Boydell Press, 2010), p. 248; 'A pretty but not a merry show', *The Times*, 21 December 1965.

13 David and Caroline Stafford, *Fings Ain't Wot They Used to Be: The Lionel Bart Story* (London: Omnibus Press, 2011), p. 191.

14 Ken Mandelbaum, *Not Since Carrie: Forty Years of Broadway Musical Flops* (New York: St Martin's Press, 1992), p. 341.

15 Mandelbaum, *Not Since Carrie*, p. 146.

16 R. Dawkins and T. R. Carlisle, 'Parental investment, mate desertion and a fallacy', *Nature* 262 (8 July 1976), pp. 131–3; Richard Dawkins

and H. Jane Brockmann, 'Do digger wasps commit the Concorde fallacy?', *Animal Behaviour* 28, 3 (1980), pp. 892–6.

17 Osborne, *Almost a Gentleman*, p. 118.

18 Potts, *Dante Called You Beatrice*, p. 104.

19 Potts, *Invitation to a Sacrament*, p. 66.

20 Jeffrey Bernard, 'Anticipatory', *Spectator*, 14 October 1978, p. 28.

21 Jeffrey Bernard, 'In all sincerity', *Spectator*, 11 December 1982, p. 34.

22 Joseph Mitchell, 'Joe Gould's Secret' in *Up in the Old Hotel and Other Stories* (New York: Vintage Books, 1993), p. 693.

23 Potts, *Dante Called You Beatrice*, p. 105.

24 Potts, *Dante Called You Beatrice*, p. 105.

25 Rebecca Solnit, *Hope in the Dark: Untold Histories, Wild Possibilities* (Edinburgh: Canongate, 2016), pp. 65–6.

6. The Crooked Timber of Humanity

1 Raymond Carver, 'Fires' in *Fires: Essays, Poems, Stories* (New York: Vintage, 1989), p. 33.

2 Bruce Weber, 'Raymond Carver: A chronicler of blue-collar despair', *New York Times*, 24 June 1984.

3 Penelope Fitzgerald, *The Bookshop* (Boston: Mariner, 1997), p. 107.

4 D. W. Winnicott, 'For Stepparents' in *The Collected Works of D. W. Winnicott, Volume 5, 1955–1959*, ed. Lesley Caldwell and Helen Taylor Robinson (Oxford: Oxford University Press, 2016), pp. 57–8.

5 Anne Boyer, *The Undying: A Meditation on Modern Illness* (London: Allen Lane, 2019), pp. 76, 239.

6 Melanie Stefan, 'A CV of failures', *Nature* 468 (18 November 2010), p. 467.

7 Michael Hamburger, *A Mug's Game: Intermittent Memoirs* (Manchester: Carcanet Press, 1973), pp. 292–3; Diana Athill, *Alive, Alive Oh! And Other Things That Matter* (London: Granta, 2015), p. 2.

8 Seymour Krim, 'For my Brothers and Sisters in the Failure Business' in *Missing a Beat: The Rants and Regrets of Seymour Krim*, ed. Mark

Cohen (Syracuse, NY: Syracuse University Press, 2010), pp. 184–5, 178, 186.

9 Martha C. Nussbaum, 'Transcending Humanity' in *Love's Knowledge: Essays on Philosophy and Literature* (Oxford: Oxford University Press, 1992), pp. 365–91.

7. The Republic of Failure

1 Ursula K. Le Guin, 'A Left-handed Commencement Address' in *Dancing at the Edge of the World: Thoughts on Words, Women, Places* (New York: Grove Press, 1989), pp. 116–17.

Acknowledgements

I almost failed to write this book, just as I failed to write the one before it. So thank you to the friends, family and colleagues who helped in various ways and enabled me to finish it: Elspeth Graham, Lynsey Hanley, Jan André Ludvigsen, Filippo Menozzi, Liam Moran, Glenda Norquay, Joanna Price, Joe Sim, Gerry Smyth and Karolina Sutton. Special thanks to Wynn Moran and Kate Walchester for reading a draft version and making helpful suggestions. Emma Horton copy-edited the manuscript with great care and sensitivity. Daniel Crewe was a wonderful editor, as ever. All the book's failures remain my own fault.

The book is dedicated to Jo Croft, dearest friend and very successful human.

Index